INVADED BY GOD

A return to faith

JACK CLEMO

Marshall Pickering

Also by the author:

Wilding Graft (Chatto 1948, Mott 1983)
Confession of a Rebel (Chatto 1949, 1975)
The Marriage of a Rebel (Gollancz 1980)
The Bouncing Hills (Truran Publications 1983)

Poetry:

The Map of Clay (Methuen 1961)
Cactus on Carmel (Methuen 1967)
The Echoing Tip (Methuen 1971)
Broad Autumn (Methuen 1975)

Marshall Morgan and Scott
Marshall Pickering
3 Beggarwood Lane, Basingstoke, Hants RG23 7LP, UK

Copyright © 1958 and 1986 by Jack Clemo

First published by Lakeland in 1972
This edition published in 1986 by Marshall Morgan and
Scott Publications Ltd
Part of the Marshall Pickering Holdings Group
A subsidiary of the Zondervan Corporation

British Library CIP Data

Clemo, Jack
    The invading Gospel: a return to faith. — 3rd ed.
    1. Converts
    I. Title
248.2′46′0924   BV4916

ISBN 0-551-00239-5

Printed and bound in Great Britain by
Anchor Brendon Limited, Tiptree, Essex.

CONTENTS

PREFACE
to the Third Edition

The ultimate purpose of an invasion is the establishment of peace following the triumph of the invader. No Christian testimony would be complete without the note of serenity, and I do not want the theme of this book to give a one-sided or distorted view of Christian experience. A life of perpetual inner tension and conflict would indicate religious neurosis rather than the indwelling of the Holy Spirit, and any attempt at outreach which lacked sympathy, compassion and general goodwill would show a faulty understanding of the mind of Christ. If our surrender is genuine, we do reach a point where — as I once put it in a playful diary parody of Kipling —

"The tumult and the doubting dies,
  The carpings and the kinks depart".

Some people may get rid of the doubting long before they get rid of the kinks, but this will depend largely on the sincerity of their desire for fellowship. The individual personality is developed and liberated in the state of grace, but it is in the hands of an omniscient God who arranges the contacts and friendships which, if we respond to them rightly, will enable us to function in our true place within the Body of Christ, happily and lovably normal.

Though I was a non-churchgoer until I married in middle age, my sensitivity as a poet provided an area in which I could learn the humility that is the key to inward peace. Having committed myself to the Head of the Church, I was no longer in collision with unpoetical and unimaginative believers. I came to revel in books and magazines which displayed a crudity of style that would have jarred on my natural taste — testimonies from spheres quite alien to me. I felt a startling and satisfying sense of brotherhood with converted sportsmen, businessmen, politicians, scientists and entertainers. They showed me that Christ was at work in the ordinary world of plain newspaper facts as well as in my private romantic labyrinths of subtlety and symbol. The feeling of spiritual unity, transcending all barriers of temperament, was a precious gift. If I had any suspicions, they concerned the poet's tendency to treat facts as mere mental images around which the fancy could play while the ego remains unyielding. Thus Walter de la Mare had written:

> *"No map shows my Jerusalem,*
> *No history my Christ".*

This retreat into a subjective religious dream, an ideal fantasy, is the cause of much mystical perversion. It generates a spurious tranquillity and complacency which rejects the discipline of Christian tradition and substitutes "dialogue" for Gospel preaching. The unity of all types of character in Christ has no kinship with the benevolent mix-up of carefully selected fragments of all faiths, since the "Christ" in such fragments is not the Christ of history. He is a figure whom Hindus and Buddhists can imagine and admire as a guru, and whom Moslems can associate with their delightful myth about the archangel Gabriel bringing a flower from Paradise so that when the Virgin Mary sniffed the heavenly perfume she conceived a son. Myths are more charming than the bare facts of the Apostles' Creed, and they may seem to offer more stimulus to poets, but they cannot channel salvation to anyone.

During the 1970's and early 1980's there was rather too much emphasis on "dialogue" and not enough proclamation of the redemptive "foolishness of God" on which St Paul insisted. A sharing of the natural spiritual wisdom of mankind became fashionable. The growth of charity between different denominations and different religions was deeply moving, a welcome change from the old fanatical hatreds which had erupted in religious wars and the horrors of the Inquisition and the Crusades. But a vague concept of divine love, and a re-affirmation of the universal human search for truth, eclipsed the Gospel challenge in some areas of both the Protestant and Catholic sectors of the Church. At its worst this was a limp concession to humanism; at its best it was a sincere attempt to distinguish between eternal reality and temporal modes of expression.

I was tolerant but unconvinced by these visions of a vast, harmonious spiritual kingdom to be attained through the suppression or "mythologizing" of Biblical facts and doctrines which embody the Christian fight against error. I was willing to admit that Christ is active outside official Christianity, and that the wind of the Spirit blows where it lists. I believed that grace can operate where the word "grace" is unknown — as it was unknown to the dying thief on the cross. But I was also aware that the peace which Christ gives is not of the world, nor of the world's religions. It is not the mystic hush of the Eastern ashram where men of diverse faiths sit and meditate, any more than it is in the Western arts clubs where the reading of obscure poetry sends people to sleep. The pursuit of beauty, or even prayer, beyond the frontier of the intelligible, cannot identify with the Christian peace that passes understanding, for it lacks the paradox which bases peace on sharply-defined certainties that the awakened conscience once understood too well for its comfort.

I matured into my sixties within the New Testament pattern of rest after divine conquest. Sectarian pride and prejudice had never meant anything to me, and without making any conscious effort to be ecumenical or broad-minded I found myself co-operating with Christians in many churches — Baptists, Pentecostalists, Salvationists, an Anglican bishop and a Roman Catholic poet. After my wife and I moved from Cornwall to Weymouth in 1984, our active gestures of faith were almost entirely Evangelical, including participation in the naval Bible fellowship at Portland. My closing symbol of peace in a dark and chaotic cosmos may therefore, very aptly be, the barbecue which some of our members organised on stony Chesil Beach one summer night. The sun had set, the joyous gospel choruses drifted softly along the shore, while the glow from a brazier lit up the quiet incoming tide. We had all submitted to an invasion, we were all relaxed, and neither the scene nor our mood could be called religious.

Jack Clemo
Weymouth
1985.

CHAPTER ONE

EXILE

*He hath no form nor comeliness: and when we shall
see him, there is no beauty that we should desire him.*

Isaiah

*Nearly they fell who stand,
And with cold after-fear
Look back to mark how near
They grazed the Sirens' Land.*

C. S. Lewis

I

It is sometimes said that the intellectual pilgrimage is the
hard way to faith. Those who take it are inclined to be
scornful of conservative believers who humbly accept an
authoritative creed and then seek only the unfolding of
truths they have already received. My own youthful
search for God was intuitive and emotional rather than
intellectual; it involved a much fiercer conflict than a
mere worry over doubts, but it had the same basic flaw as
the search of the cold, logical thinker. It was an arrogant
quest for self-fulfilment.

I became a non-Churchgoer in my early teens, not because I was indifferent to religion, but because I had
become spiritually unsettled, isolated by the need to find a
personal approach to faith. In Victorian times my family
had produced three Methodist ministers and a
local preacher—my grandfather—who once travelled
from his Cornish claywork farm to Plymouth in order

to hear Torrey, the famous American revivalist. Tradition had therefore set me amid Nonconformist simplicity, the fervour of village Bethels and mass evangelism. But the natural piety I may have inherited from these sources was offset by a restless Bohemian streak I had derived from certain members of my father's family. I had to fight among the clay-kilns and refuse-burrows of mid-Cornwall the same sort of battle as D. H. Lawrence fought among the headstocks and slag-heaps of the Derbyshire collieries. Though I had published fiction and verse before I was fifteen, I knew I could never be satisfied as a mere artist. I was always trying to open up something beyond art. But the theological keys supplied by "progressive" Nonconformity were not rigid enough to turn the lock: when I endeavoured to use them and enter the presence of the ultimate mystery, they merely changed shape—the door was still shut. I therefore left these limp and repulsive keys and began to spend my Sundays on the clayworks where everything was rigid, fantastic in its white lunar sharpness. I tried to make a spiritual key from the industrial features, and the process helped to fashion me a poet. It was soon challenged, however, by a more normal symbol of ultimate mystery—the "eternal feminine" with its incalculable moods of fluidity and tension. My inner world became complicated by the clash of images and loyalties: the chapel, the clay landscape, the perilous frontiers of sex.

When young people break away from the Church it is usually because the pagan element in them has recoiled from the Christian atmosphere. Jesus as the "good magician", so fascinating to the child mind, has faded into the nursery world, and something else emerges, something which begins making demands and offers which they resent. They may be inarticulate about it, but their feeling is similar to that of the hedonistic poets. The shadow of Swinburne's "pale Galilean" has touched their nerves, threatening their self-expression, their instinctive affirmation of life. They are dimly aware of the conflict between nature and grace, and however much the grace may be diluted or disguised by youth workers, it is still recognized by the young as an alien force. They see that the Christian definition of "love" is alarmingly different from the natural one. Even if they are only told to love God and their neighbour, as long as they attend Church and hear the Bible read they will be reminded that this is not the whole reality. Christian love has something to do with a Cross. The unknown potential of God's love for mankind, for themselves as individuals, is poised against them. In the Church, God loves them in a unique way, and it is a way which offends them because it is so largely concerned with their guilt. The "loving heavenly Father" becomes ambiguous, no longer a tolerant nature deity whom their hearts could applaud, but a vague menace incarnate in a martyr. The aroused ego turns to the world or the earth for refuge, seeking some fresh clue to natural religion or following the obvious clues to irreligion.

My dominant urge was to escape from reason into the dark shrine of erotic mysticism. The social gospel and liberal theology can provide nothing to suit the taste of such a man; but neither can the orthodox Faith. It solves his problem only when he responds to the demand which it makes of him and the rationalist alike—the demand for repentance. I evaded this demand and hoped to find a solution that would be neither irreligious nor cramping to my personal freedom. I occasionally sought clues in the Bible, but found little help except in the Old Testament with its fiercely elemental vision and primitive love stories. There was not a single love story in the New Testament, no Christian counterpart to the Song of Songs. Christ had kept the sex relation curtly out of His parables, which presented only the bond between rulers and subjects, masters and servants, fathers and sons. His few references to sex were shrewd rather than mystical, and were chiefly negative. Where was the reputed excellence of Jesus as a religious teacher? Had not Solomon and Hosea embraced a more poignant and vital truth? They certainly understood and valued the subtle emotional power of woman's love. Christ apparently did not. Even His talk with a prostitute sounded to me like a mere theological debate which He had won by an assertion of racial superiority: "Salvation is of the Jews!"[1] Why were the Gospels so austere, so lacking in recognition of the spiritual potency of "desire gratified" as Blake knew it? Only one incident, the miracle at the Cana wedding, might have offered a clue, and this was said by many scholars to be unhistorical, an allegory of the transformation of Judaism under Christian influence. If they were right, the whole character and teaching of Jesus was a stumbling-block to me—more so than that of St. Paul, for Paul did admit a little sex mysticism in his theology. But the concept of Christ as the Husband of the Church seemed remote, mythical; while the "human Jesus" was to me indeed the inhuman figure portayed by Anatole France:

> *He loves not lovers nor their bridal chaunts;*
> *He loves not love, and ever finds His good*
> *In want and thirst and barren womanhood.*

The passionate heart could only conceive of Him with fear and repugnance:

> *O Prince of death, whose cold strength serves to blight*
> *Warm love, and chill the virgin at man's breast—*
> *Thou art Divine!*

For converted young people this nightmare perversion, if it recurs at all, is usually banished by the marriage service and the exultant wedding hymns. The Christian home arises, and the radiant young parents can afford to smile at the pagan caricature. They have found that Christian self-denial is a paradox, that what seems to be its "cold strength" turns to blazing happiness when mixed with the right theology. But my circumstances laid me wide open to hedonist assault. I remained baffled and frustrated, with no personal answer to books which expressed an instinctive rebellion against Christianity: Marlowe's *Dr. Faustus*, Olive Schreiner's *The Story of an African Farm*, and the more extravagant passages of Marie Corelli: "Love! It's what the Lord Christ never knew, and where He fails to be our companion in suffering." I tried to extract a wry pleasure from the nastiest squibs of Burns, and wrote equally crude rhymes about my thwarted daydreams. The struggle between the mystic and the sensualist was intense, however, and I was sometimes driven to establish a balance through a romantic religiosity which pressed Christian symbols into the service of hedonism:

> I bridge the Fall, not by the grim
> Cold weight of creed stones lying dim
> In churches where Your folk consort—
> Folk who would frown upon all sport.
> Through live clay-rock, warm hair entwined,
> I reach back to the Primal Mind.
> My hand need never yield hers up
> To take a sacramental cup
> Or priestly bread. How could we two
> Kiss without remembering You?

But such attempts at compromise always broke down because they were based on fantasy. Objective realities were not at all like my imaginative picture of them. The inexorable Voice still challenged: "If thine eye offend thee, pluck it out: it is better for thee to enter into the kingdom of God with one eye, than having two eyes to be cast into hell fire: where their worm dieth not, and the fire is not quenched." [2]

I was worn out with this inner turmoil before I ended my teens, and during the summer months I often sought distraction by taking bus rides to one of the beaches on the nearby coast. Here were the ordinary outsiders, unentangled by the sick fancies of "poesy". I wished to feel myself in harmony with them, to be careless and relaxed in the sunshine. But I never really escaped: my personal world would not merge with the fluid life of the foreshore or with the peace of the beechwoods on the headland. I was too complex to derive comfort from Keats' sentimental dictum that "Beauty is Truth, Truth Beauty". I could only grope my way slowly and painfully along the frontiers of three realms, all of which seemed to reject me. There was the industrial clay world with its bleak, jagged symbols; the natural world, overshadowed by feminine repulse; and the religious world, in which I could hear nothing but the Voice commending eunuchs as inheritors of the Kingdom. My alienation from the Gospel was entirely emotional; it was not at all due to the broadening of my intellectual range. I read sceptical literature, but Renan, Wells and Shaw did not lead me to raise a question-mark against the authenticity of Christian foundations. I did not doubt Christianity—I merely disliked it; or rather, I disliked its façade, while being conscious that behind the façade there was some tremendous secret which I could not get at but which was the only thing that could satisfy me. The reasoned defence of the faith could not meet my need. I was indifferent to prosaic evidence; I demanded only an appeal to the primitive awareness that was making me a poet.

Many poets have an itch of irrationality in them, for poets must live passionately and this brings them into conflict with everything that would make the world safe and tidy. Their warm, haphazard way of picking up clues may be essential to their "especially privileged insight", but it may also produce an especially perverted insight, a rejection of the rational Logos. The poet is by nature a pervert, and most of the world's religious and mystical poetry is theologically heretical. The creative impulse is so easily fooled; it will function on illusion as powerfully as on truth, and therefore cannot be trusted until it has been placed under Christian discipline.

Like all forms of art, the poetic faculty is allied to natural religion—one might almost say, allied to the fertility cults. Its basic urge is to extol and interpret the moods of procreation—sexual love, the teeming soil, and the splendours of an immanent deity. If Christian truth is to capture a man of this type, it must by-pass the understanding and confront him in a manner that is at once more subtle and more wayward, more awesome and more intense. Such a temperament apprehends that the Christian God, who is said to be "a consuming fire", cannot be contacted in the icy regions of the intellect, but only along the frontiers of flamy vision.

These frontiers, however, were no longer accessible from the routine life of the Protestant Church. Its chief denominations had made a cult of the "historical Jesus", the Jewish Rabbi who had been martyred for his ideals. There was a general tendency to pare the New Testament character down to an agreeably modern core of Marxist revolt or sentimental friendliness. Such trimmings could not remove for me the offence of the Divine incognito. If the Marxist's Jesus had any fire in him, its only apparent purpose was to consume capitalism. If there was any flame in Jesus the Universal Friend it was entirely of the spirit, remote from earthly ardours. Neither of these presentations could mean anything to pagan natures who demanded the darkly fertile, the forbidden mystery. For them, I felt, religion must involve a fusion of soul and sense, a baptism or intoxication akin to the erotic. The "historical Jesus" had made no concession to this viewpoint, yet he was said to be the only incarnation of a loving creative God.

This had been D. H. Lawrence's problem, but I seemed to have already reached in my teens, and without his help—for I had then read nothing of him except a few innocuous extracts—the point he reached in *The Man Who Died*, near the end of his life. In that book he pictured Jesus as realizing at last that his asceticism had been a mistake, and that the overtones of fleshly rapture brought a revelation "beyond prayer". I had the same instinctive feeling and I do not suppose that the mere feeling made me exceptional; few adolescents would claim that saying their prayers gives them as profound a revelation as love-making. I was unusual only in being obsessed with this one question, and articulate about it. My whole time and thought were expended in the effort to find some reconciliation between Christianity and the life of the senses. The battle went on, religious fantasy clashing with brutal realism, so that I was by turns a raw artist and a bitter controversialist. I wrote fiction—later destroyed the manuscript—of sullen eroticism, but nearly all my verse showed the recurring, pathetic search for a Jesus whom I could accept:

> *Love's blasphemy is holier than a creed,*
> *Sweet with the urge of Eden's nuptial need,*
> *And when all words and altars lose their flame,*
> *Still hails the God in whom our flesh did bleed.*

These lines reveal the influence of Omar Khayyám's *Rubáiyát*, a work which I found very poignant and congenial to me at that time. He, too—and Fitz-Gerald—could affirm that "Jesus from the ground suspires", yet remain in despairing hedonism.

I was preserved from despair by the very pang of exile which showed me that the emotional assurance I was seeking did in fact exist. The pure fervour of revivalism, as I had known it at the Bethel in early childhood, haunted me still. And as I entered my twenties, the spiritual sensitiveness began to strengthen. I found myself isolated from the Churches not so much by my paganism as by my awareness of movements on the eternal frontier. I was watchful and expectant and sometimes afraid. I could not reach beyond the frontier, but something from beyond it was reaching me, leading me to recognition of the basic fallacy of the unregenerate search for God. In moments of tranquillity I caught the first gleams of the truth that finally solved my problem, the fact that the ultimate step towards Christianity is not a search but a surrender.

[1] John 4: 22.
[2] Mark 9: 47, 48.

CHAPTER TWO

THE INVADED FRONTIER

It is the road—which is the shadow cast by the Cross upon all "healthy" human life: which is the place where the tenacity of men is invisibly, yet most effectually, disturbed and shattered and dissolved; the place where the competence of God, of the Spirit, of Eternity, can enter within our horizon.

Karl Barth

Then did the Form expand, expand:
I knew Him through the dread disguise
As the whole God within His eyes
Embraced me.

Browning

I

From the Christian standpoint, every attempt to find absolute truth without submission to authority is an elaborate dodge, a laborious feat of self-protection. The New Testament reveals that human nature is devoid of spiritual life and must be yielded to God for regeneration. No faculty of mind or emotion can apprehend truth except on the basis of forgiveness for its natural alienation from truth. All Scriptural commands to "seek God" are addressed to the soul, not the analytical brain or the intuitive sense; and the soul is to seek only in the light of surrender. The painstaking sifting of evidence, the constant play of the inquiring mind, and the flights of mystical fancy, are therefore carried on in disregard of the divine revelations, and unless the unsurrendered seeker is struck down on some Damascus Road, he never reaches conversion at all. He goes through life selecting the religious ideas which suit his taste and rejecting or perverting the absolute truth which would judge and correct it. He touches only a temporal validity, a mere shadow of the eternal validity which belongs to the revelation of grace.

The keynote of this book is surrender, for that is the foundation of all Christian belief. An unsurrendered soul cannot accept Christianity, since every human personality is in its natural state anti-Christian. It is only as we submit to what repels us in the Gospel that we are given the capacity to enjoy it. Much complacency among unbelievers is due to their failure to realize this fact. Some of my literary friends claim that while Christianity seems to be the right religion for me, it would not be the right religion for them, as their temperament and tastes are so different from mine. This attitude springs from a faulty understanding of the nature of Christian faith. It assumes that I accepted Christianity because I found it so congenial to my own insight. In reality, I found Christian teaching and even the character of Jesus so repellent that I spent my teen years in wrestling with dark angels that might yield some alternative clue to the Absolute. As far as my unregenerate ego is concerned, Christianity is certainly not the "right religion" for me, any more than it can be the "right religion" for any other unregenerate soul. "The natural man receiveth not the things of the Spirit"[1]—that is still true, even if the natural man happens to be born with the so-called religious temperament. Some people are religious through stress of heredity, and there are diseases and frustrations which stimulate the religious instinct; but the consequent flurry of concern about "God" does not bring such folk one step nearer to Christian faith. The Gospel of salvation by grace, offering to raise us as fallen creatures into the power of beliefs for which we have no tastes and to which we have no right, is offensive to us all whether our natural bias is towards mysticism or materialism. Marx hurls at it his social philosophy, Emily Brontë her "celestial shine", Darwin resists it with an evolutionary theory, Emerson with a transcendental vision. Shelley screens himself from it in the mythology of ancient Greece, and Bertrand Russell seeks refuge in the duller mythology of modern science. Every temperament reveals its depravity by inventing its own alternatives, its own retaliation, its own dodge.

The need of a divine invasion follows from the fact of man's plight as a fallen and depraved creature. Many people seem to be perturbed and even dismayed because the Pauline doctrine of total depravity has been revived by some of the most influential theologians of this century. But there is nothing monstrous or misanthropic about the doctrine; it is entirely theological and has no reference whatever to moral values. Total depravity does not mean total criminality or total nastiness; it does not mean that all the people one sees in the street are feeling murderous or lustful. It means that all human beings have a strong natural objection to being justified by the righteousness of God in Christ instead of by the "good points" of nature in themselves. Total depravity means total resistance to grace and consequent inability to meet God's demand for perfection. Since God is perfect He demands that a creature made in His own image should reflect His perfection on a finite scale. When man is not being perfect he is transgressing God's law; and since the Fall he has been transgressing it all the time, in his virtue as well as in his vice, in his religion as well as in his irreligion. His highest achievements "come short of the glory of God". No one suggests that they come short of the glory of man, but in the light of absolute divine holiness the glory of man is seen to be defective and corrupted. It cannot enter the Kingdom of God, and must be overwhelmed either by His grace or His judgment. Both involve disillusion, but the disillusion caused by the triumph of grace leads to surrender; that caused by judgment leads to despair. The disillusion of the youthful Browning was of grace and therefore we have the Epilogue to *Asolando*. The disillusion of the ageing H. G. Wells was of judgment and therefore we have *Mind at the End of its Tether*.

The Christian answer to human depravity is the Gospel which blocks every avenue of man's religious search proclaiming that in Christ man has already been found, justified and received into sonship by God. The continuation of man's desire to think or feel his own way into spiritual light is thus a resistance to God's assertion that it is He and not man who is the successful seeker. The religious quest is unreal, for man is actually left with nothing to do but accept the divine verdict and be thrilled into vital experience by the paradox behind its bristling façade. The Gospel which redeems an arrogant creature must first humiliate him; the perfection he sees in Christ must contradict his own "good points". The saving truth confronts man as a barbed and fiery opposition, for that alone can rouse the alienated soul to the battle in which it is conquered by grace. The intensity and duration of the struggle varies with temperament and circumstance: the fight may go on for years, or it may begin and end while a man is listening to a sermon or reading a chapter of the Bible. The important thing is that the natural man should lose the battle and evacuate every position of self-fulfilment.

Some ministers of religion have tried to woo people into the Christian faith by assuring them that they cannot fulfil themselves outside the Church. This appeal is superficial and misleading; the deeper truth is that people cannot fully surrender themselves (in the theological sense) outside the Church. On every natural level, man can fulfil himself only by staying outside the fold of grace; but this is easy self-fulfilment; the satisfying of egotistical desire is the fulfilment of a tragic fate. The tragedy of man is that until his natural cry for "life" has been shouted down by the Christian negation, he can only fulfil his destiny as a fallen creature. If we look away from the surrendered Body of Christ we see nothing but an orgy of self-fulfilment—the gratifying of natural instincts, tastes and ambitions, leading always to a sense of futility because the achievement is not conditioned by the paradox of faith. In pursuing the obvious pleasures on the earthly and worldly side of the eternal frontier, man discovers the grim irony of his fate: it is only when he accepts the contradiction from the divine side that he discovers the joyous secret of his inheritance in Christ. The frowning Christian's façade is transformed as the shadow of man's ego passes from it. The merciless divine strategy is seen to be an essential part of the fun of salvation. God has made the way into the Kingdom seem terribly hard so that man may realize how completely his sin has separated him from his Maker. By assenting to the bitter terms of reconciliation he is brought to a perspective from which he can share the sweetness, and even the playfulness, at the heart of divine love.

2

It was in the poetry of Browning that I first found a clue to the basic Christian paradox, the relation between surrender and true fulfilment. I was switched from the simplicity and weariness of the romantic poets to the complex and strident hot-gospelling of a man who had become a great prophet of optimism in a rather mystifying way. Browning had written like a flaming evangelist at the end of a search for the fulfilment of an earthly vision—a search which he had begun as a semi-pagan mystic, a rebel against the orthodoxy of his childhood. Something momentous had happened to him on his journey from Shelley to Elizabeth Barrett, and I did not have to read far into his work before I discovered what it was. *Pauline* illuminated the whole process, showing what Evangelical conversion must mean even to a poet for whom life naturally flowers in religious symbols.

At the outset came the purely sensuous quest amid "all shapes of strange delights", culminating in the human image of Pauline, the supreme temporal bounty. But the illusion of security was soon shattered. The glow faded from the earthly paradise as the shadow of divine grace impinged, blotting out every vestige of the ideal, including the "hope of perfecting mankind" through a return to primitive simplicity. There was the conviction of sin and fear of judgment "with darkness hastening on". The human image was obliterated, and in an anguish of self-discovery the penitent turned to the divine love incarnate in Christ. The invocation "O Thou pale form" is reminiscent of Swinburne's defiant apostrophe, but here Christ is seen in the context of grace and no longer resisted. In the desperate need to be rid of "sin and lust and pride", everything else is overwhelmed as the exiled soul cries for its true home:

> My God, my God, let me for once look on Thee
> As though nought else existed—we alone.
> Take from me powers and pleasures—let me die
> Ages, so I see Thee.

Then came the moment of relaxation in surrender, the willingness to pay the price for the vision of God on the temporal level where the privilege of witness could be experienced. The most extreme asceticism was acceptable if it should be a necessary condition of discipleship.

> A mortal, sin's familiar friend, doth here
> Avow that he will give all earth's reward,
> But to believe and humbly teach the faith,
> In suffering, and poverty, and shame, . . .

And then the paradox appears, the incredible thing

happens. The human symbol, dissolved by grace for the contact of surrender, is restored; the prophecy of the earthly paradise is reaffirmed in a new dimension—still poetic, still adapted to the temperament of the convert, but purged of self-indulgence and idolatry. There is the exultant declaration of a reborn, eternal love for Pauline:

> *I shall see all clearer and love better:*
> *And beauteous shapes will come to me again,*
> *And unknown secrets will be trusted to me,*
> *Which were not mine when wavering—but now*
> *I shall be priest and lover.*

The quest was now realistic, merely for the personal embodiment of the regenerated vision. Having been found by the redeeming God, the poet was free to seek the fulfilment of His plan for the dedicated life—a plan which was the very reverse of the "suffering and poverty and shame" which had been anticipated. The sense of an earthly search in the state of grace, the knowledge that God was guiding him and had already appointed the goal, was implicit in much of the poetry Browning wrote during the ten years following his conversion. It flashed out in *Paracelsus* in such lines as "Too intimate a tie connects me with our God" and "That only way I can be satisfied". When he wrote *Sordello* he was still waiting "the first of intimations, who to love", but at last after the long testing he discovered that his voluptuous "Pauline" was a pious invalid shut up in a darkened room at Wimpole Street. This completed the paradox, showing the divine playfulness which is so utterly different from the mocking jests of fate.

For me, however, the most significant part of the whole pattern was the fact that the first poem Browning wrote after his marriage was one from which all temporal attachments were excluded that God might be all in all. *Christmas Eve* and *Easter Day* almost forestall Barth in their insistence on the transcendent "otherness" of God. Amid the rich fruition of his earthly dream, the consecrated lover must remind himself of his primary loyalty:

> Remembering every moment Who,
> Besides creating thee unto
> These ends, and these for thee, was said
> To undergo death in thy stead
> In flesh like thine.

I was startled into a great hope and expectancy as I realized that this witness to the Atonement stemmed from Browning's love-life and would never have been given if he had not married. At that stage of my development I could not have been convinced by the religious testimony of a frustrated person. I still feel uneasy about those who "escape" into divine love because they have been denied human love. Such people sometimes become saints, but more often they seek in God what they have failed to find in human beings—something congenial to their own natures, someone to "understand" and congratulate them. This merely transfers the quest for self-fulfilment to a different level and is the antithesis of surrender. The lonely and starved may have a genuine experience of grace, and it is very precious to them, but the spiritual by-products of maladjustment can never be accepted as Christian experience. I was impressed and challenged by a man who could affirm the transcendent love of Christ when all the lights of his earthly joy were steadfast and unfailing.

Browning's experience was not exceptional: it was for me only the first instance of what I later found to be the norm among surrendered personalities. Coventry Patmore, the most uxorious of Christian poets, whispered to his wife as he lay dying, "I love you, my dear, but the Lord is my light." The most emotional of the great American evangelists of our time, Oral Roberts, struck the same note when he declared from the heart of a radiant marriage, "I love Jesus more than I love my wife. She knows it and she is not jealous!" It is such men as these, not thwarted celibates, who unlock for us the paradox of the apparently monstrous Christian demand that we should "hate" earthly comforts and relationships for Christ's sake. "Where dwells enjoyment, there is He"; and though the fact that He is there as an invader is a shock, it is an oppression only as long as the enjoyment is regarded as an end in itself.

What I have chiefly learnt from Browning is that the negative approach to the Absolute is perverse and unwholesome. I had read several of the classics from the cloisters, including Thomas à Kempis's *Imitation of Christ*, and had found their cold spirituality not only repulsive to my own instincts but strangely and morbidly different from the ascetic façade of the New Testament. The self-denial which Browning advocated was quite in harmony with the teaching of Jesus and Paul. The sinner must reach a point of detachment where he sees God in Christ "as though nought else existed", and in order to bring him to this point God might allow his earthly prospects to be blighted for a while. But this was not the end of the process; it was only the crossing of a frontier, and beyond the frontier the most amazing discoveries awaited the true disciple. The outreach to the Absolute was made, not from relative starvation or satiety but from the core of spiritual self-yielding in every pure enjoyment. Nature was vilified only that the believer, at the height of his gratitude for "natural" blessing, might still be justified by grace alone.

The inability of the natural man to understand the meaning of grace is the root of the whole trouble. The wild attacks on Christianity by pagan rebels are, as far as they can see, the protests of vitality against nullity. In actual fact they are the feeble gestures of a sick creature against the infinite, though unrecognized, vitality of an alien Kingdom. Once this Kingdom is perceived by submissive faith, its tumultuous energy is liberated, sweeping away the carnal sickness in the joyous, bubbling effervescence of Pentecost. Browning often captured the zest of this unique impact: at the close of *Christmas Eve* he clutches at Whitfield's hymn-book to steady himself as he is borne beyond the shallows of poetic vision:

> *May the truth shine out, stand ever before us!*
> *I put up pencil and join chorus*
> *To Hepzibah Tune, without further apology,*
> *The last five verses of the third section*
> *Of the seventeenth hymn in Whitfield's Collection,*
> *To conclude with the doxology.*

This is Pentecostal writing, full of a spiritual exuberance too intense for art. The context shows how inevitable is the clash between Christianity and the discipline of the aesthete: "Frothy spume and frequent sputter prove that the soul's depths boil in earnest!" I was not surprised to find that this poem, which throws such clear light on the rewards of surrender, had given offence to austere critics, especially those who were preoccuped with man's religious search. Lascelles Abercrombie, in his essay on Browning, *The Great Victorian*, described *Christmas Eve* as "a doggerel rendering of abysmally dull sectarian theology, futile, small, and profitless, which can never, one would think, have had much importance, and now has none whatever". This, of course tells us nothing about Browning's poem; it merely indicates that Abercrombie did not like sectarian theology and though this was unfortunate for him it has nothing to do with literary criticism. If a poet can "conclude with the doxology" his message cannot lack importance, for he must possess something which nine-tenths of the world's poets and philosophers have sought in vain in all the territory of nature. But the standards of modern culture are perverse. They exalt the baffled seeker above the man who has surrendered to the truth and is exultantly proclaiming what it has done for him. Abercrombie went on to cite Matthew Arnold as the poet who shows us what religious poetry ought to be like. This apparently means that only poets who reject Christianity should write about religion. Those who accept the Gospel are too exhilarated by it to strike the correct "religious" note of jaded reverence and dignified despair.

I was beginning to apprehend the truth which I later found in Barth's work—that the Christian Gospel is at its deepest level anti-religious. It asserts that man is saved by the arbitrary decision of God, not by his own attempts to practise any religion, Christian or otherwise. By stressing God's search for man it forbids us to be solemn about man's search for God. It undermines our veneration for the founders of the world's religions—Mohammed, Buddha, Confucius, and the rest of the Eastern mystics and moralists who have set masses of humanity on a weary pilgrimage towards an elusive or oppressive Wisdom. As Barth declares, natural religion is a part of natural depravity, and God makes no contact with it except to bring it under judgment. In so far as Jesus Himself was a "religious man", He had to suffer frustration—not because He was depraved, but because in becoming "religous" He entered into our sin and took our infirmity. The more cultured and sensitive spirits are too often concerned with the mere religion of Jesus, claiming for it (as Matthew Arnold foolishly did) a "sweet reasonableness" which is incompatible with the Pentecostal thrill, the invading shock from outside man's spiritual orbit.

I was no longer trying to find anything agreeable to me in the Man whom orthodoxy was said to have hidden. I was too acutely aware of the God whom the cultural religionists had hidden—"this *near* God with His upsetting ways", as T. F. Powys called Him. I saw that one of the chief weaknesses of the modern Church was its embarrassment about the "upsetting" character of the Incarnation. To many ministers, Christ was apparently not so much the incarnate love of God (which can be very dangerous to the world) as the incarnate "niceness" of God (which is, of course, merely nice and not dangerous even to the religious world). They were offering a Gospel which was entirely stripped of paradox, a Gospel in which everything turned out to be just what one would expect it to be, and was therefore dull. There was no hint of the wayward process in which men must quake before they can see the joke, and surrender everything before they can really enjoy anything. The message which should overwhelm and regenerate had been so diluted by compromise that it was scarcely a challenge. The way into the Kingdom had been made to appear ridiculously easy in order to meet the supposed needs of the outsider, whose real need was to be pitched into his personal battle with grace. I was an outsider myself, aware that my pagan foundations had crumbled, that all the frontiers of my life were being invaded by a power which the Church should interpret to me. But the only Gospel which could interpret it had been effectively screened in most pulpits of "progressive" Protestantism: I had to find my clues elsewhere.

3

By the end of 1937, my Evangelical faith was stable, not a mere mood followed by pagan reaction, as it had been during the previous two years. My daily study of the Bible was becoming more and more intense and illuminating. I was spending many profitable hours with the half-dozen volumes of Spurgeon's works in my home. Despite their heavy Victorian style, they had a massiveness and a sense of spiritual authority which I found really awesome. Equally challenging, if less massive, was the testimony of great Christians who had lived and laboured in my own lifetime. Perhaps the most piquant and disturbing influence on the final stage of my surrender was

Norman Grubb's biography of C. J. Studd, the wayward cricketer-missionary, who had died only six years before. The book showed me what was involved in full consecration, a life completely overswept by the forces of the eternal world. Studd's practical philosophy was based on the belief that "God wants not nibblers of the possible but grabbers of the impossible." The Christian must renounce the tricks of self-help and self-reliance, he must lose his life for Christ's sake, and then, in the new dimension of grace, he must claim his inheritance as a child of God. For Studd, Christian experience meant pure supernaturalism, reckless gambling with Bible texts as the only guarantee of success. The disciple of Christ must step right outside "normal" procedure; he must demonstrate that he belongs to a Kingdom whose laws were "foolishness" to the carnal, calculating mind. Whether he needed health, money or wife, all motives and methods promoted by worldly wisdom and selfish instinct must be discarded; the blessing must reach him through channels opened by prayer and the direct intervention of God. The whole life must become a rebuke and a stumbling block to common sense.

The amazing way in which Studd's wild and fanatical "gambles of faith" were always vindicated did more to convince me of the truth of Christianity than any number of books on Christian apologetics. I read Paley's *Evidences*, but it meant no more to me than *The Origin of Species*. I thought it a cold, heathen sort of book. Studd himself had no patience with the academic defence of the Faith, or even with its formal presentation in pulpits. "It's experience, not preaching, that hurts the devil and confounds the world, because unanswerable; its training is not that of the schools but of the market, nothing but forked lightning Christians will count." He knew that the "forked-lightning" of Christianity lies in personal witness, not in the cool manipulation of ideas by people who are merely clever at religion. Though he was a university man, he developed something like a contempt for the intellect. "God wants faith and fools, not talent and culture," he said. "It's the hot, free heart and not the balanced head that knocks the devil out. Ours not to reason why; ours but to dare and dash forward." His soul often blazed out in prophetic rage against the cautious liberalism that was robbing so many Church members of the zest for adventure and producing "the sleepy, lukewarm, faithless, namby-pamby Christian world".

I found him a true and stimulating guide—in some ways more helpful than Browning, for he remained a firebrand to the end, while Browning's Evangelical witness seemed to function only within the orbit of his "Pauline" vision and almost faded out after his wife's death. The theme of fulfilment through surrender was dominant in them both, but presented from opposite poles of temperament and capacity. This gave me vivid proof of the universality of the Christian faith. Mysticism and philosophy are only for those who happen to be born with a mystical or philosophical turn of mind, but precisely because Christianity is outside all temperaments it can invade them all: poet and sportsman are equally vulnerable.

The fact that this breezy cricketer had such a profound and lasting influence on me showed that my Christian sympathies were becoming much deeper than my natural one. In general tastes and outlook no one could be more remote from me than Studd. He was an entirely non-mystical extrovert, and shared the usual facetious attitude of the athlete towards poetry and aesthetic values. He would have had no insight at all into the mystical-erotic struggle of my teens. Yet he pointed me to its solution, for he proclaimed the one infallible remedy for all human ills—full surrender to the invading righteousness of Christ. He kindled my determination to take the ultimate gamble, hand over my natural cosmos at the frontier, and throw myself on the mercy of God which had been so utterly veiled behind the negative façade.

It was a gradual process, a progressive yielding to the

infiltration of grace. I cannot recall any time or place where I made the final act of surrender. There were many moments when I gained a heightened consciousness of the marvellous change that had come to me. Often when I was out on the clay-ridges in the evenings, the tip-beams standing up like crosses in the fading light, I would bow my head and put the whole force of my soul into the lines of the hymn, "Just as I am, without one plea . . ." I would feel the deep tides of Christian truth flooding in over the natural defences:

> Just as I am: Thy love unknown
> Hath broken every barrier down.

My conversion was as Evangelical as if it took place at a revivalist meeting. There was nothing vague or woolly about it—no mystical fancy or romantic extravagance. I did not become aware of an Infinite or a Whole or a Cosmic Consciousness. I believed what the Bible said about Christ and human nature, and let the collision between His grace and my own nature smash the pagan tragedy to which I had been doomed. I accepted the forgiveness of sins and the authority of the Word, that was all. I have no other basis of philosophy or speculation to offer in this book—nothing but the Gospel of invading grace with all its transfiguring paradoxes.

1 Corinthians 2: 14.

CHAPTER THREE

THE CLOISTERED WITNESS

Thou shalt be His witness unto all men of what thou hast seen and heard.

Acts, 22 15

I—prison-bird, with a ruddy strife
  At breast, and a lip whence storm-notes start—
Hold on, hope hard in the subtle thing
  That's Spirit: though cloistered fast, soar free;

Browning

I

An individualist might be expected to disagree with Wesley's view that the Bible knows nothing of solitary religion. There would seem to be Scriptural evidence to support such disagreement. Christ spent forty days in the wilderness, alone with God and the devil. St. Paul after his conversion "went away into Arabia" to brood like an anchorite. But the individualist would have to admit that in each case the solitude was only a phase of preparation. Christ came back from the wilderness to fulfil His ministry among the crowds. Paul returned from the desert to stir up tumult in half the cities of Europe. What Wesley meant was that the Bible knows nothing of solitary religion as a goal, and this is obviously true. The Bible is largely a record of mass movements; it is on the whole a turbulent and noisy book, quite free from the sluggish spirituality of the East. Even St. John's Epistles show a bristle at heretics here and there, and they are immediately followed by the fierce onslaught of Jude and the lurid melodrama of the Apocalypse.

The message of the Bible is that man lives by sensationalism alone, for every word of God is a sensational word. His most secret whisper must be "proclaimed from the housetops". He startles and contradicts the individual soul, and when the soul has surrendered it is used to startle and contradict other people. There is the divine urge towards publicity and promulgation: the invading Voice continues to smite and various cultured and disgruntled voices are heard trying to smite back. A Freudian writer has complained with typical Freudian petulance, "In time, converts band together in such numbers that they, the diseased, can interfere with the healthy unconverted—and they are always anxious to do this." The statement is true up to a point, but is this petulance really healthy? At any rate, Christian converts do band together and they do make something of a nuisance of themselves in their attempt to spread the "disease". The persistence of this phenomenal irritant, divine grace, must be very annoying to those who want to believe in the orderly progress of mankind. But God will have nothing to do with orderly progress. There was a catastrophic Fall and there must be a dynamic Redemption.

In the ranks of the Church Militant there can be no room for the contemplative recluse, the man who spends his life in the effort to develop and enjoy his own "inner light". When Christianity invades, the "inner light" must be cast into the bonfire or blown out by the Pentecostal tempest. Faith must replace mysticism, and solitary brooding must give way to the tension and excitement of fellowship in a crusade. The results may alarm Freudians and other nervous persons, but Christian vision can never be "private". Even its extreme expression in flamboyant mass evangelism is better than the "reverence" of the detached seeker. There is no Scriptural warrant for a pallid and austere definition of reverence. The psalmists and prophets sometimes meditated quietly

on the Law, but when they glimpsed the coming redemption they called on the very trees and mountains to
join in their exuberance. Their imagery of hills skipping
and valleys clapping their hands is an almost frantic re-
pudiation of the sobriety and restraint of religious isolationism. A similar vitality marks the Christian
Pentecost, and it is significant that in Christ's letters to
the seven Churches of the Apocalypse there is no word of
rebuke for excessive zeal, though some of these churches
must have been, by modern English standards, swamped
in fanaticism. Christ's whip-lash was for Laodicea—the
cool, sleek, complacent religionists. Having announced
that He had come to "send fire on the earth", He could
not complain that the blaze was becoming too hot or too
dangerous. He *meant* it to be dangerous.

Occasionally this flame strikes into the literary world
and produces a Browning, a Donne or a Vachel Lindsay
—a man who uses his art, and even violates it, in the in-
terests of theological tub-thumping. Donne knew the in-
adequacy of the spiritual experience, which can only
"breathe, shine and seem to mend". In language similar to
the penitential passages of *Pauline* he prayed for the over-
throw of this mystic quietude: "Batter my heart ...
break, blow, burn and make me new!" The answer to
that prayer brought him to the pulpit of St. Paul's Cathedral and made him, as an Anglo-Catholic critic observed,
"the religious spellbinder, the Reverend Billy Sunday of
his age".

This evangelistic fervour is a part of the divine invasion; it is not, like mysticism, a diverting of natural
energies into a religious channel. The soul-moving or
"spellbinding" quality in the Christian witness—the mag-
netism which enables him to get converts—is something
unknown to him in his unregenerate state. Christ implied
this when He said to His disciples: "Ye shall receive
power after that the Holy Ghost is come upon
you."[1] The New Testament writers do not seem to have
possessed any literary gifts before or after they made

their contributions to the inspired Word. Outside the Bible, natural gifts are used in Christian service, but they are charged and motivated by a driving-force from beyond this world—a potency absorbed through Scripture, prayer and communion. This "filling" by the Holy Spirit must not be confused with the creative processes of sublimation, which have no kinship at all with divine grace. Frustration may stimulate the artist and mystic, but it can never release or increase the converting power of the Gospel.

The relation between art and evangelism is an important and neglected aspect of the Christian impact on society. Individualism has to reckon with Pentecost. Art is the product of individualistic vision which is rooted in loneliness, often in arrogance and suffering. Evangelism is the product of Pentecostal exhilaration which banishes loneliness and arrogance and is entirely devoid of the stimulus of misery. The evangelist is therefore the instrument of a rival creative energy, always poised with the threat of aggression on the frontiers of human self-development. The world of culture cannot ignore the evangelist, for in the long run public taste depends on the success or failure of contemporary evangelists. The moral and aesthetic tone of every age is determined by the number of people who accept the eternal perspective as Christ revealed it, and it is the evangelists, either as speakers or writers, who first make average outsiders aware of this perspective. When evangelists fail to get much response, the popular demand is for everything that reflects spiritual weariness, moral decadence and intellectual distortion. When they succeed, the general taste is for all that reflects the buoyancy and vigour of a living faith. Christian revival exposes the dullness and futility of unbelief, and a culture which continues to express unbelief will cease to make contact with the awakened masses.

I already felt—and feel much more strongly today—that it is good for the artist to be humbled by the achievement of the evangelist. Art finds its most satisfying level when it is content to be a footnote to spiritual renaissance. There are times when a creative artist wakes up from his dreams and wants to be a life-changer, but if he does not live in an age of faith he will probably get back into his ivory tower or break out into the wrong type of life-changing as a moral or political anarchist. Those who practise art as mere self-expression are always disillusioned. Thomas Hardy often complained that his art made him miserable and he wished he had never written books. T. F. Powys abandoned writing because he had found no happiness in it and had come to the conclusion that "all art is a refined decay". The trouble with both these writers was that their art was not vitalized by a positive faith. They barred themselves away from the "bright believing band" and were therefore left stranded with their own individualistic vision of cosmic tragedy.

Nothing but disaster can result from the artistic integrity which compels a man to be a detached and cynical spectator of redemption. It has blasted some of the greatest literary figures of the century and infected their work with a spiritual, moral and even mental sickness which makes nonsense of the Freudian claim about the "healthy unconverted". Whatever their temperament or talent, all men have been warned against the ultimate nightmare of self-fulfilment, and to them all there is offered but one alternative—participation in the redemptive witness of Christ. The creative spirit in both literary and plastic arts can only add to a human chaos unless it affirms, directly or indirectly, the value of a transcendent kingdom. The artist's faith must emerge from its proud solitudes and be tempered by the divine "herd instinct" of Pentecost, thereby allying the artist with the evangelist, who is always on the winning side when the Church generates an atmosphere in which he can function at full strength. The evangelist is the only rebel whose life-changing urge is valid beyond time and space, and the artist who spins his delicate fancies as an alternative to the Gospel is very likely to join the ignoble company of "martyred" egoists.

2

It was inevitable that when I looked again at the routine life of the churches from my new standpoint as a convert, I should still feel repelled by it, just as Vachel Lindsay must have been repelled by the liberal churches in America. The fact that I had found my Damascus Road outside organized religion was in itself a barrier to fellowship. Though my creed was the same as that of all Evangelicals it existed against a very different background, full of private symbols drawn from clayworks and Browning's poems. The mystical concept of the Christian as "priest and lover" had a more dominant place in my thought than it could have in the average church member. The aftermath of my battle with hedonism had taken me beyond their spiritual and imaginative range. I knew that my conversion could not be demonstrated by a subjective vision which cut me off from my fellows: Christianity was a brotherhood, a "communion of saints". But I had come to it under the burden of artistic gifts that were inseparable from a pagan and sensuous approach to life. Confronted with the obligation to "bear witness", yet cloistered by a wayward creative temperament, I seemed at times to face a spiritual No Man's Land.

I continued to spend my Sundays on the clayworks, often browsing through whole chapters of a pocket Testament as I sat on a gravelly ridge in the evenings. I would glance across the valley at the village Bethels, longing to be in the sanctuary yet finding no point of contact. In any of those buildings the preacher might be commending the pacifist views of Jesus of Nazareth or the Utopian nostrums of H. G. Wells or leading the congregation in singing some Unitarian hymn about social progress. . . . I would react fiercely, my mind smouldering and ironical. The natural primitivism was gone: there was no swamp, no pagan darkness, but grace had restored for its own use the elemental gifts I had surrendered. I knew that the drums of an invading Gospel should be sounding in these rural chapels. This was the land of Billy Bray and William O'Bryan, men who had brought the fervour of the spiritual tropics into the grey industrialism of Victorian Cornwall. But they were long dead, and all subsequent attempts to rekindle the flame had been spasmodic. Gipsy Smith had come to Cornwall during my teens with something of the old spellbinding throb, but the enthusiasm had soon cooled and he had gone back to America. Even there the excitement of full-blooded belief was dwindling and confused for want of leadership. Billy Sunday was dead, and so were Vachel Lindsay and that shrill, garish tub-thumper, Aimée Mac-Pherson (who was at least more reverent than the High Critic). The pure forests of the Lord seemed to be growing silent, the graves very still. I felt myself to be alone with a vision, with the vibrating energy of a music for which no one else of my generation had any taste or capacity.

I had to find my affinities in books, and therefore largely ignored the brilliant intellectuals of the day. I knew what they stood for, and left them to rot amid their own fireworks while I basked in the spiritual light which flowed from the pens of Harold Begbie, Hugh Redwood, A. J. Russell, S. D. Gordon, Dinsdale Young, Lionel Fletcher, Edwin Orr, and other Evangelical writers whose work was unknown to the Bloomsbury élite. Begbie's *Broken Earthenware* had fascinated me when I first read it in boyhood, and as I struggled back towards Christianity in my late teens I had tried to find some clues in its graphic record of Salvationism invading the slums, transforming burglars and boxers, drunkards and prostitutes. The robust Redwood and the psychic Russell showed me that I was not the only modern author who made a full surrender to the "simple Gospel", though Fleet Street journalism was very different from creative art. The American S. D. Gordon was more of an artist: he had the eccentricity and occasional childishness of a poet, and a beautiful reverence for sex. The others were rather tame compared with the old fire-breathing revivalists, but they all had the warmth of intimate contact with the Bible.

There is nothing to be surprised at—and certainly nothing to regret—in this immersion in Evangelical witness. If the intuitive writer does not submit to the stimulus of Christian revivalism, he will turn to the darker elements of the occult—to diabolism or séances, to Yoga or Rosicrucian, or to Isis and Madame Blavatsky. Such a mind cannot breathe the air of cool rationality; it can only function in an atmosphere of mystery, peril and numinous awe. It cries with W. B. Yeats:

> God save me from the thoughts men think
>   In the mind alone;
> He who sings a lasting song
>   Thinks in a marrow bone.

Like Yeats, I prayed that I might remain to the end "A foolish, passionate man".

The issue involved here is not simply the clash between the poetic and prosaic temperaments. It indicates the need and the conditions of an inspired witness. The prayer I have just quoted would have been prayed by Moses and David, Isaiah and St. Paul. It means escape from the cold cloisters of the intellect to the fertility of a live message. Nothing has done more to devitalize the Church than the excessive veneration of the intellect. The authority of scholarship has been used to intimidate church members and get them to abandon truth which an enlightened spiritual vision would confirm beyond doubt. The appeal to "intelligence" is always irrelevant where eternal verities are concerned. Christ taught that these are "hidden from the wise and prudent" and revealed to those who take the approach of "babes"—the immediate, instinctive grasp of the "born again" soul to which all knowledge is rapture. He declared that the object of His mission was emotional—"that my joy might remain in you and that your joy might be full".[2] St. Paul also stressed the emotional aspect of faith: he frequently urged believers to rejoice, to be fervent, "singing and making melody in your heart to the Lord".[3] He even advised his Greek and Roman converts to express their faith with a "Holy kiss". The voice of cold reason, glumly bidding us to weigh the evidence, is never heard in the New Testament. The idea there set up is not a man sitting with puckered brow and chin cupped in hands, mournfully pondering the riddle of existence. The New Testament idea is a man standing with face upraised and the doxology soaring from his lips. The Church cannot add to its knowledge or power by speculating about God's philosophy, for He has none. God is Wisdom itself, and therefore He does not have to think about wisdom but only to communicate its vitality—a vitality which is "unto the Greeks foolishness" because the Greeks (the intellectuals) are such a very perverse people.

Today, after eighteen centuries of cumbrous learning and scholastic debate, the Church has almost lost the naked and ecstatic apprehension of the Word: only Evangelicals retain it in Protestantism. Many ecclesiastics seem less concerned to sing a "lasting song" than to sneer at the crude theology of those who are singing it. They have abandoned the Christian ideal for that of rational religion, and regard the emotional assurance of faith as a menace. Theologians with dry, analytical brains are exalted as the most reliable interpreters of the Bible, though they have nothing in common with the strange, primitive, fiery men who wrote it. The ebullient revivalist, the naïve believer and the rhapsodic Christian poet come nearer to the Hebrews' exultation, and are thus more likely to penetrate to the burning heat of their message.

I do not say this in condemnation of Biblical scholarship as a whole, but only of the arid and arrogant type which leads to scepticism. I have a profound respect for strident and volcanic scholars like Karl Barth. It was to Barth that I dedicated the poem which expressed my ultimate release from individualism.[4] But the element of shock and storm which gives Barth's work its value is akin to that of the poet and the prophet; it has a strong emotional drive and is certainly not "in the mind alone". It was Barth himself who called on Christians to regard themselves as "hounds of God", scenting eternity in the Word and burrowing fiercely through the various encrustments cast upon it by "the world of time and things and men".

I had scarcely heard of Barth at that period, but I knew that my immediate task was to build a firm theological basis for my intuition while awaiting a more congenial climate in the Church. I agreed with all I read in the books of "popular" Evengelicals, but I needed something more massive, something that would overshadow temporal life with a sense of immutability on the grand scale. During most of 1938 I tussled with the ideas of predestination and free-will which had for so long divided Calvinists and Arminians. I balanced the homely arguments of Mary Fletcher of Madaley (Wesley's first women preacher) against the relentless hyper-Calvinism of James Haldane, the eighteenth-century Scottish theologian, and found that I preferred Mrs. Fletcher. I measured the hard logic of Jonathan Edwards against the persuasive liberalism of Henry Drummond, and found that I preferred Drummond. But when I turned from Spurgeon's sermons to Wesley's I found my affinities were entirely with the impassioned, burly Calvinist.

I liked Wesley's hymns and much of his *Journal*, but his sermons seemed to be as chilled by eighteenth-century rationality as the writings of Edwards and Haldane. They failed to give me what I needed: an assurance that the lonely spark of faith which God had kindled in me would not be trampled out but nourished into a victorious flame. Wesley taught that there was always a chanciness about faith: though God gave it, He did not guarantee that it would last. The glow might be extinguished unless the convert adhered to a rigid system of self-discipline and devotional exercises almost as negative and ascetic as those of Thomas à Kempis. There was no hint of the paradox I had learnt from Browning and Studd, the pang of surrender as a pledge of eternal joy. Wesley made me feel that I might relapse into paganism under some future crisis: a jolt of circumstance might topple me back with Swinburne, Omar Khayyám and Anatole France. This possibility robbed the act of surrender of its eternal validity as a work of grace, reducing it to a temporal decision about which God could do little but hope for the best.

It was a relief to return to Spurgeon, who refused to force divine truth into the strait-jacket of human logic. He affirmed God's predestination, not as a ruthless determinism but as something that man could choose: "As a free agent, I choose to let Him choose." There was no submission to an unknown and inscrutable "Will of God", for the general character of God's choice was already revealed in His promise of "every good gift and every perfect gift". Like all the Christians who had deeply influenced me, Spurgeon was by nature a somewhat gross, brutal man, a man who hated the cloister-damps and the attempts to make Christianity an elegantly "spiritual faith". Browning's vision of the redeemed senses had its place in Spurgeon's interpretation of the text: "Yet he hath made with me an everlasting covenant, ordered in all things, and sure."[5]

This was the basis of my particular form of Calvinism—a concept in which divine sovereignty is emphasized to inspire trust and assurance, not perverted to inspire complacency or despair. The nominal church member may go through life with as little sense of plan or purpose as the ordinary outsider, but the true convert is trained for a specific place in God's redemptive strategy. This is the next step beyond surrender. God takes the former rebel into His confidence and allots to him some stretch of existential territory where he can practise the divine presence. In a consecrated Christian life all events are ordered towards certain definite objectives, which are disclosed beforehand through the Bible or direct guidance, and as these objectives are attained, one by one, the proof of divine immutability becomes overwhelming. The believer is made invulnerable to the current climate of opinion, and the general darkness and chaos of the natural sin is less and less able to obscure the tokens of the eternal Kingdom in the midst.

All Christian evidence is rooted in the personal transaction between God and His instrument—the "private" reading of circumstances in the light of a Bible text or a tenacious intuition. The danger of egoism is ruled out by the simple fact that no covenant can be made until the ego has been surrendered. Egoists merely fulfil their natural fate, and Bernard Shaw spoke for them all when he expressed his horror at the idea of "a God who strikes bargains with His creatures". It is the glory of Christianity that it proclaims such a God. The New Testament not only asserts God's existence; it declares exciting news about Him. "Faithful is He that calleth you, who also will do it."[6] This pattern is traced back to the "bargain" He struck with Abraham over a sexual miracle, the birth of Isaac; it is demonstrated in all the Old Testament heroes of faith, and reappears very early in the Gospels in the promise God made to Simeon that he should not die before he had seen Christ. At the outset of the Christian revelation we are shown that there must be a personal divine pledge before there can be a *Nunc Dimittis*.

The sense of covenant is one of the chief marks which distinguish the Christian from the mere religious man. The latter is largely concerned with abstractions—man's vision of God, man's concept of design in the universe, or the application of religious principles to social problems. The invading Gospel sweeps aside such altruistic smoke-screens; it prepares the individual for fellowship by sending him on some personal exploit that will bring more treasure to the common stock. A loyal soldier of Christ will be busied about some unique work, something which stems from eternity; he will not mistake for Christian service the humanitarian tasks that could be done just as well by a high-minded atheist. A social gospel is a good thing on its own level, but it cannot be identified with the Christian Gospel, since its tenets are already held by decent non-Christians. Indeed, it is fairly obvious that the social gospel, like the intellectual pilgrimage, is too often a dodge for those who do not want to face Christ's demand for repentance and regeneration. A man may be very sincere in advocating "Christian" principles, yet remain totally unsurrendered in his own spiritual life. Christ did not suggest that anyone needs to be "born again" in order to have a passion for social righteousness. He insisted that men must be "born again" before they can enter into covenant relationship with the Holy Spirit of whom it is said, "He will show you things to come."[7]

Every Christian is to let his light shine, coloured by the experience which has proved to him personally the faithfulness of God. For the average believer the covenant will concern answers to prayer in business and domestic affairs; it may concern the release of a blocked talent, or the taking up of some form of Christian work in defiance of doctor's warning. Since the object of the covenant is to show that God's ways are not man's ways, there is usually an element of resistance to common sense in the divine proposal. With His "chosen instruments"—the elect spearhead of the Church Militant—He sometimes strikes a bargain for the spectacular and miraculous. His covenants with Joan of Arc and Cromwell changed the destinies of nations. His covenant with Browning involved a secret courtship and elopement and brought a new, buoyant mysticism into Christian poetry and Christian marriage. His covenant with George Müller displayed the supernatural directly at work in philanthropy. His covenant with C. T. Studd restored missionary work to its primitive simplicity: no committees or salaries, only the blind gamble of divine intervention. Later still, in 1935, His covenant with Oral Roberts carried the Christian invasion once more into the fields of physical healing and psychic phenomena. Every sphere of life is disturbed by these whispers from the Unseen; there is the secret pact with God, followed by reckless action to which the world has no clue.

As I considered this teaching in its full context of Pauline theology, I found my ideas of predestination became clearer and free from the sense of menace. I saw that Christian predestination is inseparable from the faithfulness of God. Where there is a divine covenant ratified by creaturely obedience, its fulfilment is predestinated. Where there is no faith there is no divine predestination, but only the natural sequence of cause and effect which derives from the Fall and is contrary to God's will, though overruled by His infinite wisdom.

The principle of personal covenant has some affinities with Kierkegaardian existentialism, but it was for me a solution, not an inquiry, and as I had gained so much of it from Spurgeon it was a springboard for evangelism, not a cell for philosophic brooding. I had soon proved it to be as practical as the "guidance" then being popularized by the Oxford Group. A sense of vocation in witness as "priest and lover" deepened in me as various passages of Scripture detached themselves from Jewish history and became the personal Word from a dimension in which my future was already known, already complete in Christ. I felt called to be, in Isaiah's phrase "a repairer of the breach, a restorer of paths to dwell in". Orthodox truth and Christian sex values had both been breached by modern thought—decadent scholarship and decadent morality. I knew God wanted me to do my bit towards repairing these breaches, thereby helping to restore the paths of Evangelical faith and Christian marriage.

From that time onward I wrote with a new awareness of destiny and control. My so-called literary struggle became rather a struggle for divine power, which I could receive only as I trusted God

> *to smile and guide*
> *This puny hand, and let the work so framed*
> *Be styled my work.*[8]

It is very satisfying to write in this way, separated from the rivalries and materialistic pettiness of commercial authorship. The rewards are different also from those of the dedicated artist, whose life is often tragically inconsistent with his vision. The smile of God is only for the man who submits to the in-breaking Word, which opens its redemptive assault by condemning all he can do. This is the paradox of the Christian crusade. Its fiery impact destroys the dross—the natural vision of the poet, the heresy of the religious thinker—but it is only an essential discipline of the frontier. I had now passed beyond the frontier and was beginning to understand what is implied in the fact that every Christian is a co-worker with God.

3

My first public statement of explicitly Calvinist belief was made during a controversy in the *Cornish Guardian* at Easter, 1939. I had launched a breezy attack on the pessimism of the staff columnist H. J. Willmott who had expressed the general fears about the war threat in Europe and suggested that while the nation tightened its defences we should find what solace we could in the beauties of nature. I pointed out that "rhapsodies about daffodils and primroses" would not solve the problem of human depravity, that its solution lay not in spring but in Easter. There must be something wrong with Christians who become panicky under the threat of war:

"I can only assume that they believe in a God who has realized Caliban's hope that 'He, decrepit, may doze, doze, as good as die.' I, however, do not believe in a dozing God, much less a dead one. I believe in the God who died and rose again for the redemption of a certain number of people. Knowing that that was all He meant to do up to the present, and that He has done it, I cannot work up even a groan because of what the newspapers kindly tell us are ominous signs. We are celebrating Easter; and the Easter reality is yet coming to England; the Easter dynamic is going to shake the world. I mean the Resurrection.

I leave readers to judge whether this manly and vigorous optimism of our Christian faith is not better than the truculent gloom of the scoffers, or, what is worse, the whining pessimism of the half-believers. Broadminded people can never be pessimistic; but thanks to philosophy and science, free education and free speech, there are very few broad-minded people left. On every hand we are met with the wretched dribblings of minds so narrow that they can only conceive of what is happening in Europe and forget altogether what is happening in Heaven."

Had I been given time to revise this letter, I should probably have altered the reference to "a certain number of people". I had meant to say that in every age God achieves His immediate objective, the creation of an elect nucleus or bridgehead of faith from which He can reach out to "save the world". But my phrasing was confused and misleading, and had serious repercussions in later years. When my books appeared, Willmott gave them a good deal of attention in the *Cornish Guardian* and elsewhere, including an assessment of me as a "novelist-prophet" in the book *London—Bodmin* which he wrote in collaboration with J. C. Trewin; and having this letter in mind, he attributed to me a far more extreme form of Calvinism than I had actually held. My concept of election had been derived from Spurgeon, who maintained that "the doctrine of election rightly understood, shuts none out but shuts tens of thousands in". It will be noted that even in the offending passage above the tone is buoyant: it is the Calvinism of *Pippa Passes*, not that of the *Institutes*. The style showed that I had been reading Chesterton, and this was another influence that preserved me from the antinomian abyss.

It was not surprising that I should react favourably to Chesterton's work, for I already shared his tremendous zest for the paradoxical and even nonsensical aspects of faith. A burly contempt for the world-weariness of agnostics and aesthetes was growing in me, and Chesterton certainly helped to stimulate it, especially through *Orthodoxy*, that most brilliant and devastating exposure of "adult" theology and the rational pretensions which can be torn to pieces by the superior logic of the Christian "Elfland". This Elfland enabled me to glimpse the far horizons of the Middle Ages, the blend of dogma, mysticism and childlike vivacity. The weird, haunting simplicity of *The Wild Knight* was particularly fertilizing to me as a poet. Apart from a few rhymed diary entries I had written no verse since my conversion two years before, but the oblique glamorous light of medieval romanticism produced at least a flicker of creative power and I found myself writing lines unlike any I had penned hitherto:

> *Mid all the world's strange sorrows*
> *I know a strange relief:*
> *That God has kissed Our Lady*
> *And Their Son has kissed our grief.*

At first sight it may seem incredible that a man who had just come before the public as a Calvinist should write verse describing the Virgin as Our Lady. But it was not a mere sign of youthful instability. I was very impressionable and responded with vivid sympathy to every new facet of full-blooded faith. A man of imagination cannot be a narrow sectarian; he cannot burrow into a rut and blind himself to the vision of those who live by the same basic supernaturalism. The rich, glowing colour of the medieval tapestry made a strong appeal to me and increased my dislike for the drabness of modern Nonconformity with its committee-room jargon and prosaic routine. The inconsistency of my Catholic verse was verbal rather than spiritual, for the medieval spirit, purged of its excesses of superstition and sensuality, is akin to that of Protestant revivalism. I felt that both might need to be reaffirmed to challenge an age which had lapsed quite needlessly into a torpor of doubt and frustration.

[1] Acts 1: 8.

[2] John 15: 11.

[3] Ephesians 5: 19.

[4] "The Broadening Spring": included in *The Map of Clay* (Methuen, 1961). See also my poem "On the Death of Karl Barth" in *The Echoing Tip* (Methuen, 1971).

[5] 2 Samuel 23: 5.

[6] Thessalonians 5: 24.

[7] John 16: 13.

[8] *Paracelsus.*

CHAPTER FOUR

SABOTEURS AND LOST LEADERS

Jesus I know, and Paul I know, but who are ye?
Acts, 19 15

In the Church we are concerned with truth ... And truth is not to be trifled with. If it divides the spirits, then they are divided. To oppose this commandment for the sake of a general idea of "peace" and "unity" would be a greater disaster for all concerned than such division.

Karl Barth

I

On all topics in which mere human viewpoints are involved—politics, literature, art, philosophy and "religion"—the real Christian is the most tolerant of men. He cannot take human viewpoints seriously enough to quarrel about them or wish to impose his own on other people. I have never found it difficult to obey the Christian rule in this matter. My opinions are surface loyalties, sincerely held but not defended with much tenacity. In politics I consider the Right to express a somewhat more amiable form of original sin than the Left. In literature I find D. H. Lawrence more poignant than Dickens. In art I regard Picasso as a more faithful portrait-painter than Greuze. In philosophy I feel Nietzsche to be more vital than Kant. In "religion" I think Isis a more effective goddess than Mrs. Eddy. These are my opinions, and it is quite probable that I am off the mark—especially about Mrs. Eddy. And if the issue between Orthodoxy and

Modernism were also a clash of human ideas, I could approach it with the same impish detachment.

But on this subject my attitude is anything but detached; for here we touch a reality which is in a very special sense *alive*. Our tastes and prejudices break against the *"rock* of offence", the fact that absolute truth has invaded the world and demanded the unconditional surrender of "every creature". At one point in human history God made a unique revelation concerning Himself and the nature and destiny of man. Having embodied this revelation in Scripture He committed it to the Christian Church with the solemn charge that this divine viewpoint must be preserved intact against every human viewpoint until the end of time. Orthodox believers, both Protestant and Catholic, remain loyal to this charge, but the Modernists have disobeyed it in the interest of a pitifully human concept of "progress". The issue is therefore not a petty squabble between sects and factions. If the Modernist triumphed, Christendom would lose the divine viewpoint and perish in a welter of human viewpoints, political, scientific, philosophical and "religious".

I would make it clear that when I speak of Modernists I am not thinking of those moderately "liberal" Christians who do not find it necessary to maintain the historicity of every minor detail in the Old Testament. Nor am I thinking of those whose interpretation of certain ambiguous New Testament teachings—e.g. the eschatological concepts—may differ from the traditional one. By the term "Modernist" I mean that section of the Protestant Church which has abandoned the two basic truths, the Fall and Redemption, without which the whole Christian system fails to make sense.

Differences of emphasis are, of course, inevitable. Only the complete Body of Christ can reflect every facet of the divine revelation. No individual can be more than a cell in that Body, and the cell must function where God has placed it. The surrendered temperament is given back and authorized to serve that aspect of Christian truth for which it is best suited. I have never felt impatient with Christians who accept the whole Word of God but stress some angle of it into which I myself have no particular insight. As long as a man is loyal to Bible teaching he should not be criticized, even if Christians of a different type cannot share his enthusiasm for the sacramental, social or sensational application of the teaching. Mere tolerance is not enough within the Church of Christ; a loving understanding should exist in the knowledge that "there are diversities of gifts, but the same Spirit".[1] The cool, balanced theologian should not simply "tolerate" the flaming revivalist; he should help forward the victory of the flaming revivalist by his prayers. The practical believer, working on long-term plans for social regeneration, should not merely "tolerate" the brother who is proclaiming that Christ may return next week and end the world: he should learn from this brother a more urgent concept of stewardship. The old feuds over different branches of orthodoxy have gone, but there is need of a closer bond of comradeship between loyalists whose appointed tasks might seem, on the human level, almost incompatible with each other.

My own task in "repairing the breach" had set me among those who stressed the elementary fact that Christianity is a redemptive invasion of nature by the divine grace which is outside nature and therefore outside natural religion; that its aim is to vindicate the God who rejects every offshoot of man's natural enlightenment as a basis for reconciliation. The Modernist is not emphasizing some other aspect of Christian truth; he is denying *this* aspect of it, insisting that no such invasion has taken place, that no such God exists, that the whole idea is a naïve misconception based on "crude biblical literalism". We are therefore given no choice, but have to realize that invasion means heat and battle, and though the battle between revelation and natural theology is fought with spiritual weapons, the loyal soldier fights always with the apostolic aim—"that every mouth

53

may be stopped, and all the world may become guilty before God".[2] It is too late now to ask whether such an invasion is desirable or not. Mankind would have preferred to be left in peace to achieve its "brotherhood" on a purely humanist basis. In a sense, Shelley was right when he said, "But for the Christian religion, to what height might humanity have attained!" It would have been an appalling act of egoism, but if natural religion had been allowed to spread unchecked, mankind would certainly have reached it. For it is the Christian faith, and nothing else, which breaks up the process of evolution, pronouncing and enforcing the negative verdict of God upon the natural quest and the natural goal. The Incarnation occurred and eternal truth is here, alien, intrusive and indestructible.

The most important factor in shaping the history of every age is the spiritual condition of the Christian Church. God has to renew or "revive" His redemptive assault in every generation, and He can operate only through the Church militant, the sole custodian of His paradoxical judgment and His turbulent joy. The scriptures delivered to it are at once His arsenal and the guide to His unchanging strategy. Its hymns are the only effective "trumpets that sing to battle". When all its channels of prayer, obedience and testimony are wide open, a tremendous amount of regenerating energy pours through to check the evil in the world. When its channels are narrowed by unbelief and compromise, only a trickle of power gets through—enough to maintain a bridgehead for the Kingdom (God sees to that) but not enough to prevent the mass of mankind from fulfilling its tragic fate to the uttermost.

Some extreme conservatives have claimed that if there had been no Higher Criticism there would have been no World War. They may well be right, for it was the German schools of Biblical criticism led by such scholars as Schleiermacher and Harnack, which damaged the machinery God would have used to supply Europe with His antidote to the war fever. Power-lust, fear and racial tension can be dissolved only as masses of people surrender to God's decision, the "scandal and offence" of justification by faith. By distorting the object of faith and removing the offence, the Higher Critics weakened the converting power of belief. They spread throughout Europe a profound distrust of the written Word as a weapon of grace. Its truths were haled before "a new tribunal . . . higher than God's—the educated man's", as Browning ironically observed. Even before the first World War Protestantism was ushered into the squalid era in which a man could no longer believe his Bible without being accused of "Bibliolatry", "obscurantism", "anthropomorphism", and the like. The effect of these tactics was to turn thousands of potential heroes of faith into hesitant, bewildered creatures who could not strike a convincing blow for the divine viewpoint. There was thus no dynamic Christian stand against the very human view that powerful nations should attack small nations. The later Barthian reaction against liberal and romantic theology was firm in its resistance to Hitler, but it affected only a minority of German Christians and most of the official Church leaders continued to vacillate on a basis of shallow idealism.

All through the second World War I was preoccupied with conditions in the Church, the need for Evangelical revival. The world disaster burdened me chiefly as a by-product of spiritual sabotage. I knew that the essential battle was for the souls of individuals and the ultimate redemption of the wrecked cosmos. Political and social changes caused by war or even by the adoption of Pacifism, were a mere superficial tinkering while the laws of nature and human nature remained undisturbed. And there was no sign of any such disturbance where Modernism ruled the Church. There was only the glib patter of religious salesmen. . . . Mass evangelism based on literal interpretation of the Bible was—thank goodness—a thing of the past. The traditional Gospel of personal salvation had been abandoned, for it answered questions which no one was asking today. People were no longer concerned about their sins or their souls; they wanted plain, practical religion. The modern outsider was a complete materialist, and the Church must evolve a materialistic programme if it was to make contact with the man in the street.

This had been the stock jargon along the whole Modernist Left Wing ever since my childhood. When I was a pagan mystic I had loathed it for temperamental reasons; now that I had some grounding in theology I could see how pitifully defensive it was. Certainly the average outsider was not asking, "What must I do to be saved?" but even the Philippian gaoler did not ask that until an earthquake threatened to engulf him. Since man is depraved, he will not ask ultimate questions until he is dislodged from temporal illusion. The Church's first task is to effect this dislodgement through prayer and the dynamic preaching of the supernatural Word. And it is not surprising that religious spokesmen who find this task beyond their capacity should pretend that it represents an obsolete concept and turn to social reform to create a little disturbance on the temporal plane. If a preacher lacks the power to convince his hearers of eternal punishment he may well think it best to give them his opinion on capital punishment. This evasion of fundamentals leads to a degenerate type of evangelism, the appeal of which is that of a human point of view. The unconverted are merely urged to use their natural gifts in support of the "Christian way of life", and that is still a human viewpoint, even though Jesus of Nazareth may have given it—or some aspects of it—His approval.

It is not enough that the Church should go out to the world with general religious truth; the Church must go out to the world with the truth which is exclusive to Christianity—the unchanging viewpoint of God. Church warfare is not a part of the general struggle between good and evil; it is far more complex. It attacks what is obviously bad in man and society, but only as the outworking of the paradox of surrender. At its deepest level Church warfare is a unique battle between divine grace and human "goodness", between God's merciful decision to come to man's rescue and man's innate conviction that he does not need to be rescued. Conversion is impossible until the attachment to temporal illusion and security has been smashed, and it can be smashed only as individual men and women are made to feel the tremor of cosmic disturbance which emanates from the Cross. The Christian ethic may disturb the conscience; it cannot disturb the cosmos. When Christ said, "Love thy neighbour as thyself", the cosmos did not seem to be shocked or even much interested. When He said, "My God, why has Thou forsaken me?" the shock of His words produced an earthquake and a solar black-out and ripped the veil of the Temple in pieces. The big guns of the divine invasion had opened fire on the fallen world of nature and religion.

All Church activity which does not transcend natural and religious objectives is therefore sub-Christian. A gospel which can achieve its ends without Pentecostal baptism is spurious. And as I studied the English churches during the war years I could only conclude that too many of them were functioning on this sub-Christian and spurious level. Natural theology in the pulpit, natural religion in the pew, were accepted as the normal thing in some denominations. Conciously or unconsciously, they were obstructing the advance of the eternal gospel from its awesome and miraculous bridgehead. The most prominent tools of sabotage were those I had noticed in my teens—the materialistic "social gospel", just mentioned, and the sentimental cult of the "transforming friendship". Both these heresies showed that when the authority of the Bible was denied, all sense of proportion vanished. Christ's preliminary remarks were offered as His complete message, His incidental gestures were presented as the main drama of the Incarnation.

The travesty of facts was most apparent in the popular

commendation of Jesus as the Ideal Friend. The friendship of Christ is certainly essential to the building up of Christian character after conversion, but the exponents of this cult preached the friendship itself as the converting agent. Human nature was pictured as a flower that opens in the sunshine of Christ's radiant personality. Such an image had no foundation in Scripture or experience. My own nature had been a nettle which tried to sting the sunshine, and according to the Pauline Epistles all unregenerate humans are like that. A miracle of grace must change the nettle into a bud of heavenly vitality before it can respond to the smile of the heavenly Friend. There is no historical evidence that Christ's friendship transformed anyone: if it had, the Crucifixion would have been impossible. He may have wished to challenge people by the divine purity of His spirit, but the only result was that His disciples "forsook Him and fled" and His enemies spat in His face. In the gloom of Calvary all hope of saving men by showing them a beautiful Pattern was extinguished, and if Christ's mission had meant nothing more than that, His name would be unknown in the world today. The Modernist idea of offering a simple "friendship" instead of a complex redemption was an attempt to by-pass the Atonement, the terrific point of collision between divine justice and human guilt. The element of danger was removed. The predicted Messianic cyclone had arrived as a gentle zephyr. Evangelist and missionary were merely to pass on Christ's kindly understanding. . . .

Those who tried to turn Christianity into a hard political faith or a soft, boneless humanism were fond of pointing out that Jesus Himself did not ask anyone to accept a body of orthodox doctrine. No, He did not—because orthodox doctrines are the "things of the Spirit" which the natural man cannot receive and which the disciples themselves could not receive while they were mere Jewish followers of a Jewish teacher. Jesus as the Rabbi of Nazareth did not talk to Christians. There could be no Christians before there was a Church, and this was founded at Pentecost by Peter, to whom Christ said a few hours before His death, "When thou art converted, strengthen thy brethren."[3] As a convert, a Christian, Peter strengthened his brethren on the doctrines of grace and remission of sins. In one of his Epistles he referred to Jesus not as a social reformer or an indulgent Friend, but as a Bishop, an ecclesiastical authority. The invasion was getting under way, becoming more intricate. It was a strange irony that the "progressives" wished to advance the Church by putting Christian teaching back to its most rudimentary stage, the stage in which it was not sufficiently developed to be the basis of a Church at all.

Whatever position they took up, the opponents of the absolute revelation claimed that they had honest doubts and intellectual difficulties which debarred them from assent to the traditional Christian concepts. But I had learnt from experience that such an excuse is never valid. I might have gone through life as a mystical pervert, pleading that I had temperamental difficulties which made me unsympathetic to orthodoxy. It was when I realized that *every* temperament is hostile to orthodoxy and that this is one of the chief proofs of original sin, that I found the clue which brought me in a few months from the creed of Swinburne to the creed of Spurgeon. A similar change would take place in any sceptic if he would quit dodging and face the human situation as it really is. No amiable whimsy about a "loving heavenly Father" can dismiss the fact that man as a natural creature lies under divine condemnation and can escape from that condemnation only by ceasing to be his natural self. To retain natural doubts and prejudices on the ground of "honesty" is merely to show that one's honesty is under condemnation. Every loophole has been stopped: the redemptive menace of God besets us on every side, and our only hope is in submitting to conversion at every level of our personalities until we are completely mortified to nature and vitalized by the invading Truth.

The gulf between organized religion and my personal faith seemed to widen as my artistic powers matured. In some of my writings I almost implied that the grace of Christian dogma was an elemental wind of the Spirit which blew where it listed, needing neither altar nor ritual, neither pulpit nor pew. This was an extreme and erroneous fancy, but I had to protect myself, the wound was so deep. I knew that my only true spiritual home was in the Christian communion, the affirmation of "one Lord, one faith, one baptism". Even though I had been an outsider when the great paradox of redemption dawned on me, the voice that brought me to surrender had come from within the sanctuary. Spurgeon's voice had thundered from his Tabernacle pulpit. C. T. Studd's voice had rung out from the mission field. Browning's voice had reached me from the little Calvinistic chapel where he had made that very wonderful confession. 'The giving out of a hymn reclaims me"—a line which, when one considers its theological implications, is more profound than anything in Shakespeare. This unique profundity was the goal towards which I strove. But the way to it was barred by the flood of trivial and complacent religious thought which, as Barth said, was still "bursting all dams". A prolonged friction and deadlock of this sort imposes an unbearable strain. It drove Kierkegaard near to insanity and would have unhinged Spurgeon but for the constant support of his wife. There is a psychic element in such a struggle which makes it entirely different from resistance to social injustice or political tyranny.

It may seem that I took an unnecessarily pessimistic view of the situation, and that I was not such a lone literary champion of orthodoxy as I supposed. C. S. Lewis's *Screwtape Letters* had made thousands of people face the possibility that heretics were victims of demon-possession, and that the various fashions of the "histori-cal Jesus" ("which we intend to change every twenty-five years") emanated not from ripening spiritual under-standing but from hell. I welcomed Lewis's popularity and referred in a Press controversy to its significance in relation to the half-empty churches: "Instead of going to church to hear preachers deny the Atonement, the exist-ence of the devil and the reality of hell, people stay at home and read writers like C. S. Lewis who reaffirms these supposedly outworn tenets of the Gospel." His exposition of the theological bearing of "immortal longings" in the individual had some kinship with my belief in the per-sonal convenant; it suggested that even the dons were beginning to revolt against the soul-deadening idea that a "Christian social order" was the chief object of the Incar-nation. There was little in Lewis's teaching with which I disagreed. He was no Calvinist, but Calvinism is a state-ment of how Christianity works, and fellowship rests on an agreement as to what Christianity is. On that point I was entirely at one not only with Anglo-Catholics but also with Roman Catholics. Even as a Calvinist I was not an anachronism: Niebuhr's *Nature and Destiny of Man* had appeared, showing that neo-Calvinism had found another massive and scholarly supporter.

Yet the sense of loneliness remained. A few orthodox voices from the cool halls of learning seemed remote from the clay-waste in which I was bogged, and equally remote from the flaming temples of revivalism which I longed to enter. Dorothy Sayers could present the Gospel in piquant drama, but she was coldly rational compared with Elisabeth Barrett. Niebuhr was no Vachel Lindsay, and though C. S. Lewis was a true poet, with a great breadth of imaginative sympathy, he was romantic rather than primitive. My problem could only be solved by a widespread Evangelical awaking, a mass movement in which I could sink my individualism and witness as a comrade in a victorious assault.

What cut me off from most intellectuals in the Church

and the literary world was the simple fact that having surrendered to truth I was no longer seeking truth. The Christian, like his Master, is exempt from seeking truth in order that he may seek men. My baffled search was for kindred spirits who were not themselves baffled seekers of truth. In all the coteries of culture a certain amount of spiritual paralysis was regarded as essential to a balanced faith, essential to art. But while I conceded that a paralytic cannot run wild and thereby spoil an intellectual or aesthetic pose, I took this to mean that a paralytic cannot be a crusader, a seeker of men. At the time of my conversion I had felt a climate "where spirit's spring runs wild with flaming pledge". But this had drifted down to me from the great days of Evangelical revival: the grey winter of scepticism now hung over most sections of the Church and the literary world, and in my isolation I was becoming chilled, groping for fellowship towards writers who were akin to me only in temperament.

I sometimes turned to the work of the erratic Welsh genius, John Cowper Powys, who had been reared in the Evangelical tradition but had broken away because he could no longer respect a Church which "substituted ethics for angels". I agreed that angels were more important. This eldest of the Powys brothers interested me chiefly as an illustration of the terrible price the Protestant Church was paying for its "progressive" ideas. The rare prophetic souls, yearning to prostrate themselves before supernatural mysteries and manifestations were driven out of Protestantism by its obsession with the commonplace, its mundane practicality. J. C. Powys had veered first of all to the Roman Catholic Church, but finding its moral restrictions irksome he had disintegrated into a misanthropic egoist, giving full rein to erotic mysticism and occultism. He had turned back to ancient Celtic deities, worshipping sticks and stones and "coloured angels" and "the Mohawk in the sky". I enjoyed his Rabelaisian sallies at Modernism, but his affirmations of Christian truth were so histrionic, so confused by mythology, that they could not be taken for sincere beliefs. The disciplined Christian could only feel repelled by the feverish voice babbling amid the Welsh hills: "He will come, my friends, he will come. Jesus Christ will come. King Arthur will come. And it will not be a happy day for *all*."[4] Here was the tub-thumping eloquence and fervour of a great revivalist functioning in a hollow travesty of revivalism because it had not been surrendered to Pentecostal stimulus. Had I read J. C. Powys during my teens he would have influenced me deeply, but now, even in the somewhat debilitated spiritual condition in which I spent the later war years I could make little sympathetic contact with his strange, flickering insight and hysterical power.

I felt a closer bond—for a time—with his brother, Theodore, of whom another member of the Powys family had written: "He is hunting a wild bird indeed, a bird that flies zig-zag. He is hunting God." This quest has led him outside the Church into the pantheistic vagaries of a rural recluse, but he retained a fine moral integrity and a wistful love of the Bible similar to Hardy's. What I found in his work was Christian tradition trying to express itself through a pagan temperament, becoming warped and distorted in the process. Some of the distortions were horrible and I shrank from their blasphemy, but I had written on such equally perverse things in my youth and understood the painful tension from which they were wrung. I recognized T. F. Powys as a great soul, though a stricken one. He had much in common with his ancestor, William Cowper, but he never gained the same degree of surrender. Cowper wrote lines that were completely orthodox and therefore triumphant: Powys never did. The spiritual structure of all his novels and parables is false: one only has to apply to it a few Bible texts and the whole thing comes crashing down to the level of mere art. Yet one reveres the débris, for it indicates the failure of a man who might have been an outstanding prophet if he had realized that "this *near* God with His upsetting ways" is also a God with a fixed purpose Who demands the loyal, resolute co-operation of those whom He disturbs. In the best passages of *Soliloquies of a Hermit* he did apprehend Christ as the invader of the soul:

> *"I will take Him, and all the rest of the heavenly host can go, and He will not refuse to come. All the deep thought and the dread marvels of God can go; all the hidden fears and these secret terrors can go. With the Son of Man beside me I can defy the moods; and even the old devil will cast his darts at me in vain.*
>
> *It is impossible for me, who am only mortal, to keep away from the Son of Man; He is always ready to come in, and I am not able to shut Him out; He will not allow me to put Him away; He comes in because it is His right; He comes in because the heart of man is His home."*

Had Powys always written on this level he would have taken his place beside Bunyan; but it is only a "believing mood". A few pages further on the mood has vanished, he is again in the wilderness, wrestling through sand-storms of blasphemy and crying out that he is being crushed by "the fierce coils of the immortal snake". His work can have little value for those who seek spiritual guidance; it can only be appreciated by readers who have endured a similar conflict between the spiritual and the pathological, and to those in whom the struggle has ended in a clear victory for faith, Powys will be an object of compassion rather than admiration.

I was glad to find, when I visited him in 1950, that he eventually outgrew the morbidity which clouds his books. By that time I had outgrown it also, and in recent years I have come to feel that his influence on me during the dark days of the war and its aftermath was not altogether a good thing. It retarded my advance towards fellowship with wholesome believers, and made me more sympathetic to the "brooding hermit" rôle than a healthy Christian can be. I was driven to Powys in my recoil from the ecclesiastical saboteurs: there can be little doubt that if the churches had still been ablaze with evangelistic fervour I should not have developed much taste for the primitivism and defensive irony of his work. So deeply did it move me at that period that I wrote on the flyleaf of his *Soliloquies*:

> Better be crazed with isolating Fear
> Than sane in brotherhood's pale unity:
> Stronger than team-work is the lonely tear;
> Greater than fellowship is agony.

This shows that I was in danger of becoming once more a tortured individualist instead of a loyal soldier of the Church Militant. It is impossible to say where the process might have ended if God had not supplied an effective antidote in the resurgence of American revivalism. It was the dynamic impact of the Billy Graham crusades that finally rid me of any sense of kinship with the Dorset hermit and restored me to the perspective I had held so clearly just after my conversion. In literature, as in the pulpit, Christianity should be presented with the passionate drive of the crusader, not in the hesitant tones of one still floundering in uncertainty. A man is spiritually unfit to write books as long as he is a baffled seeker. The sick soul needs health before it needs self-expression: that is basically the Christian case against "art for art's sake". The man of weak will, attached to Christ only in religious moods which he makes no effort to defend or stabilize, can never take his place among the heroes who have fought the good fight and kept the faith. He can only be pardoned as a lost leader, "still bidding crouch whom the rest bade aspire".

[1] 1 Corinthians 12: 4.
[2] Romans 3: 19.
[3] Luke 22: 32.
[4] *Autobiography.*

CHAPTER FIVE

THE THWARTED EARTH

*Because thou hast hearkened unto the voice of thy
wife, and hast eaten of the tree . . . Cursed is the
ground for thy sake.*

Genesis

*When Adam ate the irrevocable apple, Thou
Sawest beyond death resurrection of the dead.*

C. S. Lewis

I

A Christian can never be the sort of "primitive" who
tends towards nature-worship and deplores the encroachment of industrialism on the simple dignity of the
earth. He is more likely to agree with W. H. Auden that
the "ideal scenery" consists of "tramways and slag-banks,
bits of old machinery". This does not indicate a bias
towards materialism, but is entirely in accordance with
Scriptural teaching. To the prophet Ezekiel a machine
vibrating with noise was more "alive" than a flower,
more suggestive of the kind of energy that was to challenge the world through Christ. The Christian faith did
not spring up spontaneously and gracefully from our
natural soil; it swung over the eternal frontier like a celestial machine—"a Holy Ghost bulldozer", as Oral
Roberts calls it—crunching and grinding its way through
all that is natural to man, yet leaving in its path, not a
chaos of mangled ideals and shattered lives, but the miracle of the New Creation.

When we consider its eternal implications, Christianity is the most massive and awesome thing on our planet. As the divine negation of all creaturely "goodness", it is terrible. But it is also paradoxical, and those who are on the right side of the borderline between nature and grace will discover truths very different from the ideas of conventional piety. The image of the machine may be supplemented by other metaphors which reveal the total opposition that precedes total redemption. Christianity may be God's austerity breaking in upon Vanity Fair; but there is something other than Vanity Fair in our environment. There is a creation in which "the grass withereth, the flower fadeth", and in which a corrupted Life Force produces the horrors of the jungle, the asylum, the hospital and the graveyard. In relation to this grim terrestrial tragedy the impact of Christian faith is reversed. It might even be said that Christianity is God's jazz breaking in upon the mournful music of the spheres. Poets and naturalists can make us poignantly aware of that sad music, but only the Church, its Scriptures and revivalist hymns can communicate to us the invading staccato rhythms of the Celestial City.

It is significant that those who feel a divine awe in the presence of the Life Force are the very people who are appalled by the Gospel which advances with the urban stridency of banners and trumpets, neon signs and advertising campaigns. The further they retreat into the solemn mysteries of nature, the more hostile they become to the "vulgarity" of redemption. Their sensitive egos are offended: they are afraid that their most sacred altars will be kicked over—as indeed they will. Christianity is out to smash "every high thing that exalteth itself against the knowledge of God".[1] It is out to smash every natural expression of man's religious instinct: for there is nothing in man more dangerous or potentially destructive than his religious instinct. It is the root of all his sin, for a man without a religious instinct would be incapable of sin. The Christian revelation gets at the source of his perversity by attacking that which seems to him most holy and sublime. God's grace imparts a vitality which is, from the standpoint of natural religion, artificial and even blasphemous. The Gospel is a redemptive blasphemy against man's loyalty to his own ego and the evolutionary process of which it is a part. It is therefore impossible that Christianity should be solemn and reverent in the same way as natural religion: that would mean collaboration with the enemy. Even in the Church sacraments the blessing received by the communicant is not that of bread, wine and water put to a "religious" use: the transubstantiation or symbolism derives from the invading Kingdom, and the worship it evokes has nothing in common with that of the pantheist.

The snag about the spiritual use of natural beauty is that it tends to drug the conscience and destroy the sense of sin, thereby making Christian salvation seem irrelevant to the nurture of the soul. In these post-war years, as more and more of nature's marvels have been disclosed, a feeling of religious awe and wonder has arisen in multitudes of non-churchgoers. They have been driven to a vague belief in a Creator. Superficial observers have hailed this as the long-awaited spiritual revival. But the tragic thing about this uprush of "faith" outside the churches is that it is entirely naturalistic in its theology and therefore naturalistic in its morality. It has had no effect, and never can have any effect, in checking crime and divorce, juvenile delinquency and other symptoms of original sin. Where these evils have been checked, all the credit must go to Christian evangelism, which has compelled people to face the fact that the sense of wonder cannot be redemptive unless it is preceded by a sense of guilt. The only redemptive wonder is that expressed in adoration such as Crashaw's:

> Lord, what is man? why should he cost Thee
> So dear? what had his ruin lost Thee?
> Lord, what is man? that Thou has overbought
> So much a thing of nought?

This is the sense of wonder in the state of grace, the supreme reality. Its counterpart in nature is at best an illusion and at worst a disease. To feel utterly at peace, at one with universal beauty, without a flicker of repentance or recognition of grace, is to be spiritually paralysed. Most of mankind had sunk to that level when Christ came to stab men awake by His terrific insistence on the need for regeneration.

The pagan piety induced by sense impressions has led hardened sceptics to make fools of themselves, but it has never converted them. Voltaire was once so moved by the grandeur of a sunrise over the Alps that he fell to his knees and cried, "O Thou great Being!" But that brought him no nearer to Christianity than if he had derided the splash of colour in the sky. Christianity knows nothing of a "great Being" in the Deistic sense. It knows only a righteous Father, an atoning Son and a convicting Spirit. Nowhere in nature is there clear evidence of any of these three Persons: the Trinity can be known only through the Church which He created as His sole instrument of revelation. Christians who claim to find the true God in nature are reading into nature ideas they have derived from the Bible: they are seeing the fallen earth as if it were already lit up by its ultimate redemption in Christ. This is legitimate to faith, though there is always a danger of slipping into sentimentality, as some hymn-writers have done:

> Heaven above is brighter blue,
>   Earth around is sweeter green:
> Something lives in every hue
>   Christless eyes have never seen.

Many converts have felt this thrilling awareness of a transformed world, but it is a projection from their own experience of grace and therefore unrealistic. Under the bright blue and amid the sweet green, the deadly struggle for existence is still going on: animals, reptiles and birds are fighting and killing each other, shrieking against the Christian creed, as Tennyson said.

When nature-lovers boast that they can apprehend God without the aid of a church, they are using the word "God" in an entirely non-Christian sense. They are merely stating the banal fact that they do not need the help of a church in order to feel a heathen veneration for the Life Force. Such veneration can be little more than a romantic mood, for the Life Force is involved in a tribulation which is not redemptive. It extracts worship from "serious-minded" people, then makes them its victims. Reverence turns to perplexity and dismay as the mask of benevolence and beauty is swept aside by some disaster. The Christian detachment from nature is unwittingly shown to be essential to belief in a good and compassionate God. Under the shock of earthquakes, floods, cyclones or volcanic eruptions the outsider turns to the Church and comments scornfully: "And yet you Christians tell us God is love!" Only a complete orthodoxy has the adequate reply here: "Yes, but we insist that His love is in Christ, not in nature. If you stay outside Christ you stay outside the knowledge of God's love and only see Him dealing with a monstrous rebellion—dealing with it in power and over-ruling Intelligence, but not in redeeming Love." This is what gives such tremendous importance to Jesus Christ—not that He told us about the love of God but that He *is* the love of God. To approach God in any other way than through the Incarnation is to confront an unknown Power and an inscrutable Wisdom. At that level man remains unredeemed, bogged in mystery. He can escape only through the personal Christ as the Gospel records prompt the questioning of Browning's Pope:

> What lacks, then, of perfection fit for God
> But just the instance which this tale supplies
> Of love without a limit? So is strength,
> So is intelligence; then love is so,

Unlimited in its self-sacrifice:
Then is the tale true and God shows complete.

Christ himself was obviously not at peace with nature, any more than He was at peace with human nature. He often acted in open defiance of the "majesty" of creation. When the storm arose on Gennesaret He did not bid the disciples to humble themselves devoutly before the "great Being" who was trying to drown them. He lashed back at the elements from His bridgehead in the divine Kingdom: "Be still!" To Him the storm was the work of an evil Life Force, a demonic convulsion that needed cure. All natural catastrophes are symptoms of nature's sickness—fevers, vomits, shiverings: they are not growing pains through which God is slowly evolving a perfect world, but mere reminders that we live in an enemy-occupied zone and that in so far as we are subject to its laws we share its tragedy. Christ has set an example of revolt against the sick rebel, and spiritually our revolt can be an exhilarating success. We can transcend our bond with nature, not through stoicism or courage, but through intimations of the New Creation, the Kingdom of God. We can escape, not by regarding natural ills as an illusion of mortal mind but by refusing to accept their reality as the *deepest* level of experience. Our physical participation in nature's throes can be a very shallow thing even when we are dying, just as our participation in its blind creative urge can be the shallowest aspect of sex. Death and sex are the supreme powers of nature, but grace robs them both of their pagan dignity.

The same Pentecostal power which challenges the natural dignity of art and over-solemn scholarship is also at work against the cult of blood and soil. In bidding His disciples to prepare for the coming of the Holy Spirit, Christ pointed them away from all the associations of fertility, tilth and harvest: "Tarry ye in the city of Jerusalem until ye be endued with power from on high."[2] It is doubtful whether the Holy Spirit could have manifested

Himself to men among the cedars of Lebanon, on the seashore or amid the vineyards and cornfields of the plains. God had to demonstrate that the Christian triumph means the thwarted earth, the thwarted pagan impulse, and this could not be brought home to people while they were sensitive to the grandeur and tenderness of the teeming countryside. The artificial energy of the Kingdom, its urban drive against the old fallen creation, could be recognized only if the Church was founded in a city. The Church's flame was not to be kindled by the sun, like that of heathen cults; its wind was not to be that of the natural heavens, tossing the trees and waves and flowers. The fire and tempest of the Spirit were released in a stuffy little room in the slums while the streets outside were thronged with wretched, sinful humanity. There was a black-out of natural beauty for the birth of the Church: everything that could distract the disciples by its aesthetic or sensuous appeal was excluded. Reality was narrowed down to a focal point in Jerusalem: The Christ-conscious nucleus was detached and sealed to receive the invading "power from on high", the divine contradiction of every power from below, every power from the creation around and every power from the natural spirit within.

The book of Acts is clearly not the record of a faith which drew support or nourishment from the "sacredness" of the soil: it is a turbulent story of evangelism in towns and cities. There is also deep significance in the fact that when God wished to give the Church its authoritative theology He laid his hand on the urban hustler, Saul of Tarsus, a man who has been detested by naturelovers all through the centuries. Paul was obviously insensitive to the charms of earthly beauty: one cannot imagine him stooping to admire a flower or pausing to listen to a bird singing. His epistles could not have been written by a rural dweller; they have about them the stridency, restlessness and high tension of the streets. The Christian withdrawal from the spurious "holiness" of the Life

Force is much more pronounced than the Hebrew, although, as Barth has pointed out, the psalms which extol God's handiwork in creation were meant to be accepted only in the light of the Messianic redemption. Until that redemption is consummated, the Church must hold its Kingdom apart, free from the pagan languor which infects natural religion. Most of the great Christian poets, from Dante to Chesterton, have found their inspiration amid the clamour and vivacity of crowded streets. All the great Christian revivals have begun in towns or amid the ugliness of industrialism. A rural Pentecost can only occur when dedicated Christians gather amid beautiful scenery—as at the Keswick Convention—for devotional or evangelistic purposes which transcend the concept of God as mere Creator. Such outpourings of grace in the haunts of nature-poets are rarely sustained for long: remote country churches are usually sluggish and insipid compared with the flaming little mission-halls in the slums.

2

The orthodox Christian view of "fallen nature" has often been perverted to serve the cause of asceticism. Unless its bright paradox is kept in mind it can be made to appear negative and ruthless. I have never lost sight of the paradox, but some of the work I produced immediately after the war was distorted by subjective vision and harsh symbolism, and these extravagances made me notorious as "a poet who hates flowers and all living plants, and for whom all natural life is Satanic". I am anxious that the essential truth should stand clear of personal overtones due to my lack of the discipline of fellowship.

The sense of a rebellious anti-Christian element in natural forces had been strong in me from my youth. Before my conversion I had felt it chiefly in relation to sex, but I was also aware of the corruption of the breeding earth. My later submission to Christianity did not lead me to reject temporal beauty as such: the material form and colour of plants were pleasing to me, but they existed only through the death and decay of vegetable and animal organisms. The greater the corruption in the soil, the more rank and flaunting was the growth which the Life Force produced from it, and the implications of this were entirely pagan. I found a clue to my reaction in the preface to D. H. Lawrence's *Pansies*, where he writes:

> *"Flowers, to my thinking, are not merely pretty-pretty. They have in their fragrance an earthiness of the humus and the corruptive earth from which they spring. And pansies, in their streaked faces, have a look of many things besides hearts-ease."*

Lawrence loved flowers because they suggested manure and thus gave sanction to the flowering of the flesh in moral rottenness. No Christian could sympathize with such an outlook, though few are moved to retaliate by proclaiming, as I did, that "every tree's a Judas" and every flower is a "smirking foe" of Christ.

I was always on guard against the recurrence of paganism. One of the passages which had most gripped me at the time of my conversion was the close of Browning's *Easter Day*, his description of nature-lovers as those

> *Left in God's contempt apart*
> *With ghastly smooth life, dead at heart,*
> *Tame in earth's paddock as her prize.*

These lines made me quake. They were not mere poetry, to be appreciated with the imagination; they came home to me with the convicting power of the Holy Spirit. I realized that this might well be my fate unless I constantly saw the "paddock" as a scene of invasion, a battlefield. There certainly was a ghastly smoothness in the writings of naturalists and pastoral poets. They seemed to be sunk in utter complacency, oblivious of spiritual warfare. And

I believed Browning was right in implying that a terrible shock awaited such people at the Last Judgment. It was better to take the shock now, to fight for grace against nature, while there was still time to reach beyond the divine curse into the joyous paradox of the surrendered life.

The logic of the Kingdom enabled me to maintain my witness as "priest and lover" and to fuse it even with the most extreme poetic vilification of natural beauty. An unwavering opposition to asceticism and the celibate ideal characterized all my work. I knew that the Christian approach to the Abolute is not the obvious one expounded by Kierkegaard, to whom the monastery was the "beacon light" of mankind. The true beacon light, the radiant rebuke to worldliness and sensuality, was the Christian home, the sanctuary of redeemed sex, enshrining the wayward secret of grace through which we can deny ourselves while enjoying ourselves. I had of course faced the crucial question: "If all nature is evil, how can you praise sex and glorify marriage?" But this had never been a serious problem. I was not praising the sexuality of apes or glorifying the marriage of atheists: I was writing about Christian regeneration. Sex as a mere biological function meant little to me: I followed Browning in presenting the lover as priest, interpreting the mystery of "how bodies teach me souls". Where the soul had received grace, the body became sacramental, touching realities beyond its natural context.

The idea of a sexual transmutation is symbolized in Christ's miracle at Cana and made explicit in many passages of the Epistles. St. Paul found nothing to praise in the behaviour of the earth, the birds, animals and heathen humanity, but he was fascinated by the "great mystery" of Christian marriage: "She shall be saved in child-bearing."[3] The apostle, looking out on a cosmos groaning and travailing in bondage to a corrupted Life Force, saw Christian womanhood as the one point where creative consciousness is fused with consciousness of redemption and thereby "saved" from the crude animality, the instinctive sex-terror, which the Fall has made normal to the human reproductive process. Again and again he stressed the sanctity of the redeemed flesh, its unity with the soul in membership of Christ: "Shall I then take the members of Christ and make them the members of an harlot?"[4] A close study of the Epistles had shown me that something quite extraordinary, something we can never fully understand in this world, happens to the sex-drive when the whole personality is yielded to the Holy Spirit. The righteousness of Christ as the Husband of the Church is imputed to an otherwise carnal rapture: "else were your children unclean; but now are they holy".[5] The holiness of sex exists only where the natural "unclean" striving towards self-fulfilment has been cancelled by faith. These truths need to be emphasized today when even Church members think the Christian view of sex means nothing more than a decent ethical standard. In actual fact it means cosmic revolution, foreshadowing a new earth and enabling men and women to enter, here and now, a realm of experience which is completely barred to the materialist.

In one of her love-letters Elizabeth Barrett remarked concerning the hard-headed materialism of a friend, "I should scarcely have the strength to love you, I think, if I held such a dreary creed." This clearly implies that the depth and tenacity of her love for Browning was dependent upon her Christian faith. The "strength to love", even in the amorous sense, is conditioned by creed to a far greater extent than most people realize. All divorces, separations and infidelities reveal that the natural strength of the basic attachment has been drained and the parties have nothing left to fall back on, no creed which can interpret or solve their problem. The Christian is sustained by the artificial energy of his faith, the Pentecostal thrill which overwhelms the sickness of the Life Force. By releasing the vibrations of belief he finds his fleshly desires caught up into the power of regeneration. This can occur before the desire has begun to flag, and even before it has been given the chance to kindle through a natural or worldly stimulus.

When C. T. Studd became engaged to Priscilla Stewart, he wrote to his mother concerning this fiery little missionary: "I do not love her for her pretty face; I love her for her handsome actions towards the Lord Jesus Christ and those He sent her to save." The non-Christian has no clue at all to the motives and emotions which underlie such confessions. Love a girl *physically* because of her handsome actions to Christ? The logic of this is a secret of the Christ-centred life. Christian couples are aware that the bond between them is not that of the sensual or even naturally spiritual attraction between the sexes. In a surrendered personality the hunger to learn more of Christ is far more powerful than sexual appetite. The Christian's demand of the beloved partner is not so much "Love me" as "Show me in your love what Christ has done for your instincts and emotions." As Aimée MacPherson said, Christian marriage is compounded of "Jesus, us and I". It is this insistence on the personal Christ which is so baffling to the worldly man. What can it be, he asks himself, which makes the Founder of Christianity so overwhelmingly real to modern sportsmen and tub-thumpers that they cannot even fall in love without dragging Him in. The Freudians offer some comment, but they cannot explain or defile the mystery. When they have brought out all the available slime about religious obsessions and sexual perversions, the marvel of the Christian marriage remains. The unity of "Jesus, us and I" is still there, towering like a sunlit rock above the fogs of natural instinct amid which thousands are groping their way to the divorce court.

I quote Studd and Aimée MacPherson precisely because there was not a trace of mysticism in either of them. Both were accused of vulgarizing the Gospel by presenting it in the cheap, slangy phrases of the sports field and the street. Studd described Christ as ringing him up on the prayer telephone before a campaign and telling him to "go it for a slog". Aimée MacPherson urged her converts to be "God's G-men, God's go-getters". Christians so entirely free from spiritual fuzz can be trusted to mean just what they say, and when they make their astonishing statement about their motive in marriage we are confronted with something tremendously real—something which is, indeed, the only solution to marital and moral chaos.

The basis of Christian marriage lies in the two facts: (1) the individual hunger to learn more of Christ, and (2) the limitations of individual experience of Christ. No two persons can know Christ in exactly the same way, since no two persons have exactly the same temperament or spiritual capacity. The believer's apprehension of his Lord must therefore be completed from without, not from within, and while this need is met in general by the fellowship of the Church, the communion of saints, there are elective affinities within that communion. A Christian man meets a girl whose approach to Christ has some unique kinship with his own. Something distinct about her faith—the yearning on her face or the passion in her voice as she bears witness to it—arrests him and fills him with a great longing to fuse himself with the facet of Christ which she reflects. This longing is very difficult to define; it is not mere fellowship or friendship, and it is certainly not the result of sex appeal, for if the same girl were an atheist her face and voice would never show the spiritual intensity which fascinates him. It is not her physical beauty as such which moves him so deeply, but the suffusion of that beauty by a soul which is on fire with love for his Lord. As he yields to this urge of Christian attachment it draws in his whole personality until he reaches the point where he can hear Christ say at the heart of creative nature: "Not as the world giveth, give I unto you." This is the sexuality of the New Creation, a direct product of discipleship. The man is in love in a sense which the materialist can never understand. He and the

girl are also "one in Christ" in a sense which the spiritu-
ally-minded ascetic can never understand. They are united
at a level which even the Marriage Service does not men-
tion—chiefly because the Marriage Service was designed
for all citizens of a "Christian" State and therefore makes
no special provision for couples who have been radically
converted.

There is always a divine purpose behind this sort of attraction; it is always mutual. There are no pathetic
stories of unrequited love under the personal covenant of
grace. If nature creates obstacles, they are removed by
prayer. Priscilla Stewart had not at first felt the same
bond with Studd as he felt with her. When he proposed
she gave him a firm refusal: but he merely used this to
provide further evidence that Christian reactions in their
sphere are totally unlike those of the world. He spent
eight days in fasting and prayer then wrote to Priscilla:
"Your determination is wrong and will not stand, and you
yourself will see this presently if the Lord has not shown
it to you already. I have sought His face and to know His
will, and He has led me forward, and gives me en-
couragement and emboldens me to ask definitely for
you." Studd wrote under the guidance of the Holy Spirit,
with Whom he had been in unbroken communion for
eight days, and under the impact of this invading power
the girl's instinctive aversion, or pride, or whatever it was
that prompted her refusal, collapsed. Within a few
months they were married, and just before the wedding
Studd wrote a verse which he told his fiancée to adopt as
her daily confession:

> Jesus, I love thee;
> Thou art to me
> Dearer than ever
> Charlie can be.

This playful rhyme illuminates the Christian ideal of
mortification, which is so horribly travestied by monks

and nuns and negative thinkers like Kierkegaard. The breezy cricketer penetrated to depths which are hidden from the neurotic visionaries and philosophers. True Christian mortification is joyous and even jolly; the wholesome believer mortifies himself, not with a groan but with a joke. With a gay, laughing heart Studd mortifies his male pride and renounces the first place which a husband naturally claims in his wife's affections. He is anxious to prevent their marriage from being undermined by idolatry, and therefore seeks to guard her against the solemnity of the nature-worshipper, the erotic mystic and the sentimentalist. The principle of buoyant renunciation stood every test and remained constant throughout their married life. In his old age, when he was evangelizing African tribes and his wife was running the home end of the mission, his letters to her still struck the same exultant note: "I love you for your love for Jesus."

This is what consecrated and receptive Christians mean by love, and it is what the natural man, even the natural mystic, can never mean by love. In the whole range of worldly literature, fiction and poetry, there is no hint of the peculiar sexual bond which has Christ for its source and goal. And it must be admitted that average church members do not come within sight of it. Their surrender is so incomplete that their hunger to learn more of Christ is not strong enough to counteract a physical infatuation. Some young converts marry partners who reject Christ, and though He does not forsake such converts they can hardly expect to show the world what Christian marriage was meant to be. The Christian norm is the love which is born of faith and motivated within the state of grace.

I am not writing about some twisted and abnormal experience which has come to a few cranks and oddities. Apart from the ascetic Wesley, all the great Protestant evangelists from Luther to Billy Graham have known the type of union I describe. The colouring may vary with temperament, but the Christ of Cana is always revealed. Whenever I have written on this subject my mind has not been filled with mystical fancies, but with vivid concrete facts from the lives of the great Evangelical lovers—Browning and Elizabeth Barrett, John Fletcher and Mary Bosanquet, Studd and Priscilla Stewart, Spurgeon and Susan Thompson, William Booth and Catherine Mumford, W. E. Boardman and Mary Adams, Gipsy Smith and Mary Shaw—and dozens of obscure Christians whose testimonies I have read in Evangelical papers. No one who keeps abreast of Evangelical witness can fail to note the unchanging emphasis, the proof that Christian love is different in origin and consummation from the "racial instinct" which is legalized for the benefit of society.

In recent years I have examined the teachings of American Evangelical churches, and find that their concept of the redemption of the body is identical with my own. Some of their ministers have written books on the "spiritual biology" of Christian marriage, stressing the fact that the physical union is already trans-sexual, and the biology involved is eternal and incorruptible because it is covered by the Atonement. It is also closely allied to eschatology. Oral Roberts, in his book *The Fourth Man*, concludes a sermon on the Second Coming with a passionate affirmation in which human love reaches its true setting, the unique Christian context:

"I know that my redeemer liveth, because I am personally acquainted with Him. I humbly asked Him to forgive my many sins and set me free. He did it! He did it! I know my soul is right with my Saviour. I feel His holy presence coursing through every fibre of my body. He thrills me, He lifts me, He blesses me.

My family is ready. My darling wife is also faithful to the Saviour, and my children love Jesus. We are waiting for the Lord to come."

Here is a depth and ripeness of experience which only Christians can know. The natural is swallowed up in the supernatural, the thrill of cosmic redemption is already transforming temporal values, and the domestic horizon is the vast eternal sweep of the Day of Jesus Christ.

[1] 2 Corinthians 10: 5.
[2] Luke 24: 49.
[3] 1 Timothy 2: 15.
[4] 1 Corinthians 6: 15.
[5] 1 Corinthians 7: 14.

CHAPTER SIX

THE FALLEN WISDOM

Where is the wise? where is the scribe? where is the disputer of this world? hath not God made foolish the wisdom of this world? ... Because the foolishness of God is wiser than men; and the weakness of God is stronger than men. ... God hath chosen the foolish things of the world to confound the wise; and God hath chosen the weak things of the world to confound the things which are mighty; and base things of the world, and things which are despised, hath God chosen, yea, and things which are not, to bring to nought things that are: that no flesh should glory in His presence.

St. Paul

Blow the trumpets, crown the sages,
*   Bring the age by reason fed:*
He that sitteth in the heavens,
*   He shall laugh, the prophet said.*

G. K. Chesterton

I

From a theological standpoint, those of us who grew up between the two World Wars were fortunate. We were born too late to be caught in the backwash of nineteenth-century idealism. The word "progress" may have evoked a pious "Amen" around 1900, but it prompted a cynical jest in the 1930's. We who were then adolescent had to be realistic and try to see what lay beyond the fading of the evolutionist's dream. We could no longer take scientific idealism religiously, and therefore had a much better chance of becoming Christians. Many of our spiritual leaders had taken scientific idealism very religiously indeed and therefore almost ceased to be Christians. Young people like myself who had found the essential Gospel outside the denominations were aware that Protestantism was bogged down through its attempt to advance along a wrong route and run its machinery on fuel bequeathed to it by the Darwinians and the Higher Critics. We saw that the "progressive" churches had been the victim of a gigantic hoax. They had been induced to accept scientific findings as part of divine revelation, thereby confusing the issue between the human wisdom which evolves from below and the divine "foolishness" which has pounced from above.

Central and unperverted Christianity has never tried to suppress science as such, any more than it has tried to suppress art and literature. It merely insists that an alien eternal Kingdom has impinged on the world in which these things may be legitimately practised, and that no one can enter this Kingdom through discovering or developing the spiritual values which belong to the temporal plane. As long as science keeps to her own tasks of investigating nature and inventing things for the material benefit of mankind, no Christian could regard it with an unfriendly eye. The fields of natural religion, mysticism and the occult may be "reverently" probed. Science comes under the veto of the Gospel only when it blunders over the frontier into the holy of holies, carrying its pursuit of evidence beyond the point where God has put up the "Stop" signs of the Incarnation and the written Word. The scientific spirit in its own sphere is admirable; in the Christian sphere it can be poisonous and debilitating. The incompatibility lies in the simple fact that to the scientific spirit the "uncritical approach" is the deadly sin in *every* area of human knowledge; to the Christian there is one area where the uncritical approach is the only way of salvation.

I am puzzled to find church members so anxious that religion and science should walk hand in hand, for the closer religion draws to science the further it gets from Christianity. If anyone doubts this, let him read the New Testament—and then turn to the works of those clergy who pride themselves on their scientific outlook. In the former there is the perfect harmony of something fitting in where it belongs; in the latter there is the fussiness and irritation which accompanies the attempt to make something fit in where it does not belong. For religion, as the word is used in the Christian Church, can function normally only within the area of divine grace where its natural corruption is eliminated. To co-operate with science it must leave the orbit of grace and reassert its natural corruption—its pride, its idolatry, its participation in a human quest. Well-meaning ecclesiastics did patch up some sort of understanding between religion and science, but we could not help noticing what happened to their Christianity in the process. From the Continent came a grim warning in the apostasy of Loisy. From the Anglican Church we got books which suggested that the origins of the Christian faith were more dubious than the origin of Communism or eugenics. In the Free Churches, where one might expect to find the Upper Room and the gift of tongues, we were offered the psychiatrist's consulting-room and the gift of Freudian jargon. Christianity as God's invading foolishness, His capricious and lovely world of paradox opened to childlike faith, had disappeared.

It may seem natural that a fervid Celtic poet should recoil from the cold analytical touch of the enquiring mind, but the principle of surrender is involved here also. It is as a Christian that I preserve my faith from the laboratory climate.

The Christ to whom I yielded among those Cornish clay-peaks was the wilful Being of whom it is written again and again that He "rebuked" the fixed routine of nature on which scientists base their belief in a Master

Mathematician. He filled me with a great hunger for the "signs and wonders" by which He challenges the guardians of routine. The things I have chiefly sought in history, in newspapers and in my own life, are those moments

> *When He paces our disrupted shore,*
> *Bidding His Kingdom integrate once more,*

as I expressed it in a poem written ten years after my conversion.[1]

Up to that time I had known such moments mainly in connection with my literary work—the amazing way in which God brought through supplies when nature had locked the normal and "reasonable" channels. But I was already fascinated by the stranger manifestations of Christian power: stigmata, supernatural visions and voices, healing miracles, the miraculous preservation of flowers placed on statues of the Virgin, the appearing of angels and the macabre occurrences that sometimes accompany the casting out of demons in the name of Christ. I have since made a closer study of such matters, and gratefully accept the records which seem consistent with New Testament teaching, or which—like Bernadette's vision at Lourdes—have involved a mass of facts that make the idea of hallucination untenable. I cannot treat such accounts with suspicion and reserve unless there is good reason to believe that dubious or hysterical persons have twisted the evidence. My duty as a Christian is to be on guard against counterfeits, but at the same time to welcome every thrilling whisper concerning the activities of our wayward Christian God, to be always alert with the expectancy which Chesterton had in mind when he said, "We have sinned and grown old and our Father is younger than we"—younger and therefore fond of playing pranks on people who gravely expound His "inexorable laws". This does not mean that the Christian is to be a gullible dupe; it simply means that he is to turn his scepticism on the right object—on the wisdom of man instead of on the foolishness of God. He will be very cautious about all attempts to assess Christianity "in the light of modern knowledge"; for such light is never valid in the sphere of Christian revelation. Christ taught that the natural light in man is darkness; his only true light comes from above, from the erratic flash which violated nature in the body of the Virgin.

Modern knowledge, like natural religion, can produce results which, on the temporal level, are similar to those produced by the Gospel. But the Incarnation forces us to reckon with the divine viewpoint, "the otherness" of eternity. The question to be asked regarding any human situation is not whether it is helpful to man but whether it is helpful to the unique invasion of man which began at Nazareth. Christ and the eternal viewpoint must be central. I once read in a Nonconformist paper the statement that it does not matter whether a person is rid of an undesirable kink at a revivalist meeting or in a psychiatrist's clinic: as long as he is rid of it, the divine purpose is served. Such an idea is part of the scientific hoax which deceived so many religious folk of the older generation. It can be countered only by reference to the disturbing truths at the heart of orthodoxy.

To change men's lives is not enough. The basic thing that needs to be changed in man is not his behaviour but his status before God. Human character can be changed in many ways—through psychiatry, or a happy marriage, or an operation on the brain. But whatever benefit may accrue to society through such changes, the person retains his original status as a condemned sinner. He is still an unregenerate member of a fallen race. If the psychiatrist or the wife or the operation has turned him into an extremely nice person, he will use his "niceness" to exclude the righteousness of Christ which alone is valid in eternity. The divine verdict therefore remains against him, even though he may thank God that he is now a little nearer to the human norm. The belief that the advance of medical science and the amenities of a Welfare State are part of Christian redemption is a fallacy. These things are overruled by a kindly Providence which mitigates the horror of man's natural fate, but the decision as to whether a person is or is not "born again of the Spirit" belongs to a dimension known only to the Christian Church. The regenerate believer is, of course, as grateful as any other citizen for the blessings which Providence has allowed mankind to discover, but he realizes that something more than a general Providence is at work in the Church, that something other than a human discovery has been committed to its charge.

The failure to draw a sharp distinction between nature and grace has caused a great deal of loose thinking among people who wished to be broad-minded. They lump together in an indiscriminate mess things which belong to entirely different categories. Thus they speak of the "religious experience", as if an orgy in a temple of fertility cults were somehow akin to the signing of a decision card at a Methodist rally. They speak of "spiritual healing", as if physical changes due to natural spiritual energy or darkly occult power could be classed with the miracle-working impact of the Holy Ghost. They speak of the "marriage relationship", as if the carnal union of a pair of atheists were identical with the desire of a Christian couple to penetrate the depths of Christ's redemption of the body. The only way to clear up this confusion is to get back to Christ's claim that He had not come to send peace but division; to put a sundering sword between types of motive and action which the mystic and the humanist would fuse in unity. The Christian solution is always an alternative, a resistance movement against complacent ideals and classifications. The sphere of grace remains intact, with its own incorruptible values, but there is need of a more open witness to the transcendent Kingdom which will make no compromise with the "rudiments of the world".

The practical importance of this issue is very great, for Christians can extend the Kingdom only through manifesting the exotic fruits of the personal covenant. How exotic these fruits will be depends on the intensity of individual faith in Christianity as the stumbling-block, the upsetting and dislocating factor in the midst of human progress. Orthodoxy has always maintained that angels rush in where fools fear to tread. The old saints rushed into every sphere of natural law and won tremendous victories of faith where the modern "scientific" Christian hesitates and retreats to the latest text-book on the subject. He is so afraid of developing religious neuroses and obsessions that he dare not lift a finger against the natural routine of cause and effect. This is where science becomes an anti-Christian force which must be resisted. It goes beyond the divine "Stop" sign when it tries to limit the area in which Christian faith can operate. When modern knowledge forbids us to pray about sex or the weather, or for the healing of an "incurable" disease, it must be thrown back over the frontier into its own territory. What happens in response to Christian faith can never be understood by the rational, calculating mind, for Christian faith exists only because there was an Incarnation and a Resurrection and therefore a Voice which said: "All power is given unto Me in heaven and on earth. . . . These signs shall follow. " Of the five signs listed in Mark's Gospel, four involve a breaking or suspending of natural law, and the other ("In My name shall they cast out devils") suggests a fairly heretical disturbance of darkly supernatural law. Even if some of these specific signs were temporary the principle remains and refutes the idea that God intended Christianity to get duller and feebler as it moved out across the centuries. He certainly did not mean it to turn the world upside down only in the first century and reach the twentieth as a harmless little religion, "corrected" by science and attacking natural man with nothing more ferocious than an agenda and an order of divine worship.

Christ had launched a revolutionary crusade which was to continue "Even unto the end of the world". Unbelief must be given no rest; it must be constantly jolted by the activities of an unknown, wayward, redemptively dangerous power. The shadow of God as "a bird that flies zig-zag" was to blot out the drab findings of materialism and fertilize the souls that were willing to run wild with faith. The Church was to advance and be fruitful under the bright shadow of His wings. But outside the defiant little stretches of conservative belief the fields of spectacular witness have grown barren because Church members have lost the sense of the momentous overshadowing which is the prelude to spiritual fertility. Nominal Christians have become frozen and sterile because they think it is "unscientific" to believe in miracles, "psychologically unsound" to gamble on a Bible promise if natural probabilities are against its fulfilment. When the elect begin to show such exotic fruits, their value as Christian witness is blunted by naturalistic explanations imposed from within the Church. In a popular text-book on the ministry of healing we are told that when the sick recover through Christian anointing it is "almost as great a miracle as the frost weaving ever-changing patterns on the window pane". Such reasoning is nonsense; it is like saying that when Peter walked on the sea it was almost as miraculous as when he walked down the street. But religious people who want to appear "scientific" will try any dodge before they will admit that the natural sphere has been invaded by a Power which knows no law except faithfulness to the covenant of Scripture.

It is often argued that no experience of so-called divine intervention can be outside the laws discovered or discoverable by science, for if it were, we should have to abandon the idea of a uni-verse. But in the literal sense it cannot be said that we inhabit a uni-verse. John Cowper Powys comes nearer the truth when he asserts that we are in a multiverse—a chaos of conflicting natural and supernatural forces. Christianity narrows this down to a clear-cut dualism. It reveals that there are two ultimate Beings, God and Satan; two ultimate worlds, heaven and hell; two ultimate wills, divine predestination and natural (i.e. Satanic) fate at work on the limited free-will of man. There is thus no all-embracing Law to which everything is meekly submissive. It is true that since God is stronger than Satan His providence overrules that which is not His will. But this does not alter the fact that the division and conflict exist: there is no unity or harmony, only the split cosmos in which the individual is caught between the Fall and the Redemption. Neutrality is impossible, even for the mystic who thinks he has found it in detachment. Whatever position we adopt we are poised in defiance of some kingdom and some power. To submit to God we must resist the devil. To obey the laws of heaven we must transgress the laws of hell. To be governed by divine predestination we must reject our natural fate as sinners. The scientist, working perforce without this theological background, is unaware of the fallen state of creation; he presents us with an over-simplified picture of reality, and therefore fails to see the relevance, or even the reverence, of the traditional view of Christ as the cosmic interventionist, the law-smashing "thief in the night".

Those who sneer at orthodoxy as "pre-Darwinian" overlook what is implied in God's gift of the supernatural Church. The Christian Gospel cannot be divorced from Christian cosmology. If the Christian cosmological idea of the three-fold Fall—the fall of Satan, nature and man—were not true, mankind could get along well enough with natural religion and the supernatural Church would be superfluous, like a fire-engine rushing to a spot where there is no fire, or a lifeboat battling out where there is no wreck. The whole Christian message is permeated with the urgency of rescue, with all that this implies of heroism, danger and possible casualties. When modern thought intrudes, the sense of urgency is lost, heroic soul-saving action is abandoned, and complacency is mistaken for the peace which passeth all understanding. There is the fatal tendency to regard Christianity as a part of temporal progress, when it is, in fact, God's attempt to rescue man from temporal progress and bring him to the redemptive standstill of eternity. The spiritual diseases which sap the vitality of the Church do not spring so much from what John Betjeman calls "the Protestant underworld of mad cults" as from the Protestant upper world of excessively sane cults. The fanatic who tells us that unless we can "speak with tongues" we shall be damned is not an asset to the Christian cause, but he is less harmful than the religious snob who tells us that unless we constantly revise our creed, we shall be out of date. The fanatic has become too excited over a minor detail, but he is at least aware that a redemptive standstill exists and that Christ's promise of "new tongues" is fulfilled only to those who remain loyal to the old creed. This principle runs through every branch of Christian life and thought, and its paradox is rooted in the perpetual creativeness of Scripture, the Evangelical belief that "there are more truths yet to break forth from Thy Word". Every age does need new facets and overtones of spiritual truth, but these are already latent in the Bible text, awaiting only the surrender of personalities which can reflect and transmit them. The consecration of vivacious modern personalities has shown us that there are Pentecostal jazz-rhythms in the Bible to which our forefathers were deaf. The same texts which yielded grey and sombre truths to the Puritans are yielding radiant and exhilarating truths to the Hollywood Christian Group today.[2] The fixed revelation plays baffling tricks because it is alive and fertile.

It produces obvious paradoxes in literature. All the wholesomely original religious books, from *The Pilgrim's*

Progress to *Screwtape Letters*, have been written by men who acknowledge the authority of the unchanging Word. Religious writers who think that new angles of truth can be found only in science and human progress have never produced a truly original book. Their works are the stereotyped products of competent mediocrities, without a trace of the imaginative fire and divine waywardness which characterize the prophet. The value of conservatism has been demonstrated even in my own limited sphere. My total surrender to the Bible has brought into my writings an elemental vision which critics have described as "strange", "startling", and "extraordinary"—terms which could hardly be applied to the works of the once famous Cornish heretic, Bishop Colenso, who was born at my home town of St. Austell. I have not read the books of this learned man, but I gather that his originality extended only to a mild suggestion that certain insects did not enter Noah's Ark in pairs. The time had come to correct the Mistake of Moses. . . . We are a hundred years beyond that sort of parlour game now, and the Gospel bulldozer is making things a bit more lively as it clears away the mistakes of the Modernists. The true original is always a medium conveying vibrations from another world—the world which, as Barth says, has impinged on ours only in the double miracle of "grace as revelation and revelation as grace".

Even in fiction there is evidence that people are not dated by central Christianity but by the current alternative or amendment to it. In reading novels which reflect the nineteenth-century encroachment of science on traditional faith—such books as Hardy's *Tess* and *Jude*, Mrs. Humphry Ward's *Robert Elsmere* and Hugh Walpole's *The Cathedral*—one is struck chiefly by the unreality of the arguments put into the mouths of the infidel characters. Under the impact of the new cosmology they have come to feel that Christianity is something "small and local", that the Church "will have to go" (as Jude's mistress cries hysterically) unless it unshackles itself from an "untenable redemptive theolatry". It all sounds very silly today, like the babbling of meaningless catch-phrases by people who have got lost in a fog. Now the fog has lifted we can see that it is not Christianity but the pseudo-scientific hoax that is "small and local". The robust Pauline affirmations of the orthodox characters in these novels are still fresh and vivid, expressing a timeless and universal norm.

In direct evangelism the paradox of redemptive standstill is even more apparent. True modernity, novelty of method, shock tactics—all spring from submission to the eternal norm of Scripture, not from resistance to its authority. It is the orthodox preachers who have captured the masses by seizing the most up-to-date means of high-pressure publicity. It is the Biblical literalists who have got their message across in rodeo shows, sensational films, world-wide radio networks, television and vast sports stadiums with banner texts swinging in the floodlight. And while the orthodox camp seethes with colourful and adventurous activity, the advanced scientific churchmen can do nothing but hold conferences and read dry lectures to each other like a conclave of eighteenth-century Deists. Their distaste for the vitality of literalist belief has deprived them of the inventiveness and daring of the true pioneer.

I myself recognize allegory and hyperbole in the Old Testament, but I am a literalist about the Gospels because Christianity was meant to be a shock, and the shocking element in the New Testament records and predictions is bound up with their literal interpretation. Remove that and there is nothing left which is dangerous to the natural routine, and therefore nothing left that is worth believing. The facts of supernatural reality, unknowable to science, are given to us in the Bible, and all attempts to simplify the Scriptural statements or blur them into allegory are concessions to spiritual laziness. For many church members the supernatural has been whittled down until it means only one thing—a kindly and tolerant

God. In the Bible the supernatural means Father, Son, and Holy Spirit, angels and archangels, Satan and demons—all constantly at work in shaping the lives of individuals and the destinies of nations. But the anti-literalists are too tired to grapple with this intricate cosmology and its terrifying implications. It is so much easier to talk learnedly about primitive symbols and Babylonian legends which unfortunately coloured the thinking of the Hebrew writers.

Every aspect of the clash between the eternal validity of grace and the temporal validity of human findings points to the same conclusion. In theology as in morals, we have to learn the relentless lesson which Browning emphasized in *Fifine at the Fair*:

> *So far from realizing gain,*
> *Each step aside just proves divergency is vain,*
> *The wanderer brings home no profit from his quest*
> *Beyond the sad surmise that keeping house were best*
> *Could life begin anew . . .*

"Divergency is vain"—that is the verdict which must be passed on every departure which the Church has made from the narrow text of its original mandate. Its "steps aside" into asceticism, superstition, mysticism, rationalism, scientific and political heresies—all are seen at last to yield nothing but the sad surmise that the undistorted, undiluted truth is best. The Church can bring home no profit from its wanderings into natural fields. In stooping to enquire of man it ceases to be the vehicle of the divine answer which is humanly untenable and therefore the authentic Word of God's grace and judgment. By ceasing to keep house within its wild and "childish" Kingdom it loses touch with the Father who is younger than we.

In view of the truth I have roughly thrown together in this chapter, it was fitting that one of the first rays to pierce the cloud of my individualism, illuminating my path back to fellowship with a revived Church, came from an event which the more severe religionists could not take seriously. It was the astonishing rise to fame of America's child evangelist Renée Martz, who claimed to have been converted through a vision and the voice of Jesus in a Los Angeles street. When seven-year-old Renée arrived in England in 1947 our Church dignitaries merely smiled with benevolent condescension towards an "infant prodigy", but to me with my belief in election and the personal covenant there was a profound significance in the strange "calling" of this girl. It was a sign that God was losing patience with the dreary adult outlook in religion, that Christianity as the wayward Kingdom of the little child was being reasserted. The tyranny of a hard, dry, "reasonable" faith was being challenged afresh by the foolish things and the things which are despised. The joyous effervescence of the soul-winner had begun to function in a new and startling way—a way which exposed the folly of being "serious-minded" instead of spiritually minded.

I realized that extremes often have to be corrected by extremes, and a Church which has almost gone over to rationalism may need to be purged by revival which has almost gone over to rag-time. If this is not ideal, it can at least be argued that no method of Christian witness is ideal in itself: the ideal consists of the total co-ordinated witness of all surrendered personalities, each fufilling a covenant in its own sector. Though my sector was literary, it bordered on the evangelistic zone, and the comparative silence there after Billy Sunday's death had saddened me. I welcomed the Martz campaigns, not only as a portent of the more massive challenge which has since come through Billy Graham, Oral Roberts and T. L. Osborne, but also as a warning to myself at a time when I was writing some of my most grimly isolationist work. I saw that a fierce individualism would not serve my end, and that I might need to "put up pencil and join chorus" before I could counteract the weariness of negative religious thought.

If my spiritual taste seemed to "go American" during my thirties it was because in America God had raised up the most spectacular witnesses to the basic truth of my theology, confirming my belief in the triumph of Pentecostal turbulence over man's quiet and disillusioning pursuit of wisdom. The terrific intensity of these evangelists was due to their knowledge that the Power which went into action at Pentecost was completely outside human philosophy and reason, and therefore outside the range of everything that can bore us and make us dull. The infallible Spirit of truth has been manifested, and can do no other than lead men to the excitements of infallible truth. To deny that infallibility exists on earth is to say that we are still in the grip of our fate as baffled seekers. This would imply a denial of redemption, for divine redemption can mean nothing less than redemption from fate, from the baffled search and the fallen wisdom of man.

[1] "The Irony of Election", included in *The Map of Clay*.
[2] Instances of this abound in Dale Evans Roger's *My Spiritual Diary*.

CHAPTER SEVEN

THE ROUT OF TRAGEDY

Experience strangle hope? Hope waves a-top,
Her wings triumphant! Come what will, I win,
Whoever loses! Every dream's assured
Of soberest fulfilment. Where's a sin
Except in doubting that the light, which lured
The unwary into darkness, meant no wrong.
Had I but marched on bold, nor paused immured
By mists I should have pressed thro', passed along
My way henceforth rejoicing.

Browning

I believe Thy word and will question no more from the
darkness within me, but only from the light. And
Thou, if Thou seest that I question from the darkness,
correct me, for I desire to live, and answer me only as I
question from the Truth.

T. F. Powys

I

Though Christianity is so full of paradox, it is all too rare
for an afflicted believer to reject the cult of suffering. A
soul that is much buffeted by trouble will naturally gravi-
tate towards a philosophy of tired resignation or dour
courage. Neither of these positions can be called Christian, but they have inspired a good deal of religious writing and might have been apparent in mine had not God
shaped me for revivalism rather than moralizing. I could

not deny that I had sometimes found life a crushing burden, and I acknowledged that even after conversion the process of constant surrender has its painful phases. But in all my witness there was the hint that whatever spiritual wisdom I possessed had come to me in those moments when I glimpsed the bright waywardness of God, moments when life's solemn lessons were rebuked by a divine vivacity. Suffering in itself had taught me nothing; it had merely created the conditions in which joy could teach me, and so it could never be the last word or even the vitalizing word in my Christian adventure.

This resilient faith owed its first stimulus to Elizabeth Barrett's Love Letters, which transformed my whole attitude to the place of suffering in the Christian scheme. During my early twenties I turned almost daily to these great spiritual documents written in the gloom of Wimpole Street. The stricken poetess had declared that while she herself had been forced to live "with Sorrow for a strong companion", she recognized in Browning's testimony of "unscathed happiness" a far higher order of Christian experience. She stated that though we must sometimes be refined in the furnace it is better to be refined in the sunshine, since "furnace fire leaves scorch marks on the fruit". She declined to join the ascetics with their "ignoble groaning", and her sweetly obstinate faith brought her through the dark years of trial to radiant marriage and motherhood. Her letters moved me as deeply as Browning's poems had done, and the impression was later strengthened by the Sonnets from the Portuguese, which closed her cycle of pious witness on a note so entirely different from that of the wistful sufferers, Christina Rossetti and Anne Brontë. She reached beyond them and proclaimed with the exultancy of a great lover that "God's gifts put man's best dreams to shame". I realized that she and Browning had been united to bear a unique blended witness to the Christian norm of happiness. And I felt impelled not just to echo them, but to give in my own Cornish idiom (a bit greyer than the

99

Italian landscape) the Christian answer to suffering: neither resignation nor courage, but faith in all its fullness—the faith that surrenders, covenants, endures the testing and obtains the promise, thus rooting the whole life unshakably and eternally in the faithfulness of God. Only a soul so rooted in its secret bond with God can face the tragedy of the world without despair, for the patterned life of the individual yields the only clue to the divine order which has invaded chaos.

There is no doubt that religious tradition plays an important part in moulding one's evaluation of suffering. The Brownings were Nonconformists and their letters and poetry reflected a typically Nonconformist outlook. Had Elizabeth Barrett been a Catholic she would probably never have married: she would have accepted her tragic "vocation" like a nun and rejected Browning's offer of love as a snare of the world and the flesh. My own philosophy has been formed almost exclusively by Nonconformists—men and women who by-passed the cloisters and went straight to the Bible for their yardstick. This has often made my reactions puzzling to Christians reared in a more austere tradition.

A cultured Anglo-Catholic friend once suggested that God's will for me might be a life of unrelieved privation and loneliness. She had noticed that my early autobiographic writings were largely a record of misfortune: though it should have been clear that this was due to my pagan background and temperament and had no kinship whatever with my destiny as a Christian. But the alien pressure was still being allowed when I first met this friend in 1949, and she was therefore inclined to think that God might mean me to be totally frustrated in this world so that I might obtain some greater spiritual blessing in the next. She saw me as an embodiment of the ascetic ideal of the suffering saint, and even compared me with Bernadette. But my wayward clues had been intensified through a very different type of child visionary, Renée Martz, and I would make no concession to Catholic notions of lifelong penance and purgatory. In reply to a letter in which my friend expressed deep sympathy with me in what she called "all these disasters", I wrote obstinately: "I want my Christian friends to share my own buoyant confidence in the God who 'giveth us richly all things to enjoy'." This showed her that I was incorrigible, and she had to leave me to my Evangelical exuberance.

A robust insistence on the victory of faith for earth as well as heaven had been obvious even in the work that was warped by my isolation from the Church. The idea of the personal covenant on the *Pauline* pattern was always at the back of my mind and steered me out of the shadows as well as the shallows. In the opening stages of a spiritual or emotional venture based on the divine covenant there may be great darkness and perplexity, with the temptation to see nothing but "all these disasters", but as the believer learns to "march breast forward, never doubting clouds will break", there comes—often quite suddenly—the fulfilment of the faith which has been maintained in the days of testing:

> *His clenched hand shall unclose at last,*
> *I know, and let out all the beauty.*

That was Browning's assurance during his thirteen years' search for the appointed "Pauline". No experienced Christian would deny that there are times when God's hand is clenched, the promised blessing withheld and concealed. These are trying periods—until the believer dares to look above the clenched hand of God and catch the twinkle in His eye. After that transfiguring glimpse the journey is lightened: the eager soul presses on through the returning mists, the ironies and "satires of circumstance", knowing that even while these things are permitted, the beauty he desires is ripening in the hand of God. Under the divine covenant there can never be a plan that miscarries or a dream that does not come true. We suffer disillusion and disappointment because so much of our planning and praying is done outside the Christian covenant: in the context of nature. As Torrey put it: "When our prayers fail it is because they are indeed *our* prayers." When hopes and plans collapse it is because they are natural, unsurrendered. A life lived wholly within the orbit of grace would show an unbroken rhythm of prayer and answer, promise and fulfilment, grafting and fruit-bearing.

2

In the sphere of religious experience there are two classes of people who are to be pitied—those who remain complacently on the surface and those who get bogged in the dark enigmas just beneath the surface. The surrendered Christian penetrates below both these levels and discovers a faith that is more radiant than that of the thoughtless, and more profound than that of the serious thinker. He passes from bright and fluffy illusion into "that depth of conviction which is so like despair", but as he learns more of the paradox of grace he emerges into the eternal glow of that depth of conviction which is so like frivolity. And it must be said that those who fail to break through to this exhilaration are exposed to great danger. Some church members have ended in asylums because when calamity struck them, they were still at the intermediate stage, the level of solemnity. They began brooding about the mysterious dispensations of Providence the inscrutable ways of the Almighty, and so on; and the human mind was not meant to stand much of that sort of thing. The right way to deal with the counter-attacks of fate—and certainly the only way I have survived them myself—is to disregard them in the intensity of one's foreknowledge of deliverance. This foreknowledge is possible only when the soul is rid of all natural religious reactions, either superficial or austere, and brought into unquestioning submission to the promises of God's Word.

The Christian resistance to the tragic view of life is, of course, bound up with the concept of Christianity as an invasion from a world of infinite joy. The natural man, especially the more sensitive and poetic type, can be educated through misery because he is part of the evolutionary process when it is under divine condemnation. But the Christian has been reclaimed from that process and cannot be educated by the same means. He cannot evolve painfully from one stage of spiritual development to another; he can only grow in grace through the "immortal longings" which are stimulated by the triumph of the eternal over the temporal, which ultimately means the triumph of God's jazz over nature's "Dead March". The believer is not to share the sadness and weariness of nature, but to impose upon it the redeeming vitality of grace. His existence has value only in so far as it is lived in the Kingdom of heaven, which is the kingdom of the little child and therefore the realm in which suffering is instinctively renounced as abnormal. Such a man cannot ask solemn questions about life; he is too astonished by the wonders of the invading Kingdom as they flash and reverberate around him, now clearing the highway, now blocking a false path, now bringing him to a standstill so that he may read his Bible in a new light.

All healthy Christian witness refutes the idea that faith in Christ makes no change in the believer's circumstances but merely gives him strength to bear the common lot of mankind. If that were true, Christianity would be a mere religion, not an invasion. Religion accepts the dark mystery of life and is content to be "reverent" about it; the invading Gospel blasts the dark mystery and makes us reverent only about the joyful mystery of being saved. The thrill that surges through the Pauline Epistles and the great Evangelical hymns is that of a unique and marvellous release from the natural darkness, the common bondage. This is, indeed, just what we should expect.

When a liberating force enters occupied territory it does not give the enslaved people the strength to bear the oppressor's yoke; it breaks that yoke, brings the people under new laws and establishes their lives on a different footing. So it is with Christian faith: "If any man be in Christ he is a new creature: old things are passed away."[1] Old habits of thought are shed, and then—sometimes after a long testing, sometimes very rapidly—there comes release from emotional frustrations and entanglements, financial troubles and physical maladies that would warp the vision or block the path of service. The covenant of redemption offers nothing less than this, but the average church member lives far below the privilege of the covenant. He has never really grasped the fact that the frontier between time and eternity has been breached for him as an individual, that the wayward and miraculous power of the Incarnation has flooded through, capable of turning his world upside down and shaking the tragedy out of it.

My wide reading in biography had confirmed my view that Christian faith restricts and finally annihilates the area in which tragedy can operate. I had noticed that while the instruments of creative nature (the poets and artists) were usually overwhelmed by catastrophe, the instruments of grace (the evangelists) were strangely immune from such horrors. One cannot imagine Moody and Sankey starving in a garret, or Billy Sunday blowing his brains out. Wesley was the only evangelist who made an unfortunate marriage and even he cannot be called a tragic figure like the eighteenth-century artists—Romney, Hogarth, Chatterton, Christopher Smart and John Clare. The suggestion that great Christians are great sufferers is not borne out by the facts—certainly not in the English-speaking Protestant world. Catholicism has a morbid streak which allows the shadow of the Cross to obscure the Pentecostal exhilaration, thereby distorting the Christian ideal of saintliness. In contrast to the Protestant norm, it is the great pagans who are the great sufferers.

No modern evangelist has endured such martyrdoms as were meted out to D. H. Lawrence. Compare Lawrence's pitifully thwarted life, his changing career, his tormented wanderings around the world in a vain attempt to gain converts for his "Rananim" cult—compare this with the triumphal march of Billy Graham, and the difference between the pagan and Christian patterns is clearly manifested.

It is the difference between the genius and the apostle. With the former, the man creates the faith and therefore it will not work; with the latter the faith creates the man and works through him. The unhappy Kierkegaard recognized this, but he remained a genius and never gained the liberty of an apostle. For the apostle is vitalized with joy by the spiritual truth which is using him. He is not a "religious thinker", but a medium for the thought of God, which is already in print in the Bible and will make no compromise with the fatal "originality" of the creative human spirit. It is significant that while there is never anything of the brooding philosopher about the evangelist, there is often a touch of the showman and even of the comedian. This is as it should be, for Christianity is not God's lecture: it is His Big Show and His biggest joke. The Bible brands the solemn pomp of moral and intellectual rebellion as "filthy rags", and we can be stripped of these rags only by the Pentecostal gaiety. The element of aggressive cheerfulness in revivalism, so far from being tawdry and decadent, is an essential part of the Christian deliverance from the fever and exhaustion of egoism. It takes us to the very heart of the paradox of divine joy. The great revivalists have gone out to the world as sunny ambassadors of that Christ whose mask was the Man of Sorrows but whose unveiled face was that of one "anointed with the oil of gladness above thy fellows".[3]

I had observed also that when a creative genius surrendered his gifts to the service of alien Christian truth he escaped the divine judgment on unregenerate nature and shared the blessing of the apostle. Browning, Tennyson and Patmore stood clear of the black tide of tragedy that submerged almost all the non-Christian poets and artists of their day. Browning was most confident of his exemption from tragedy when he came nearest to the revivalist mood—as, for instance, in *Pacchiarotto* with its burlesque Calvinism:

> I'm pious
>
> However: 'twas God made you dingy
> And me—with no need to be stingy
> Of soap, when 'tis sixpence the packet,
> So dance away, boys, dust my jacket,
> Bang drum and toot fife—ay and rattle
> Your brushes, for that's half the battle!
>
> I've seen you, times—who knows how many?—
> Dance in here, strike up, play the zany,
> Make mouths at the tenant, hoot warning
> You'll find him decamped next May morning;
> Mine's freehold, by grace of the grand Lord
> Who lets out the ground here,—my landlord:
> To Him I pay quit-rent—devotion;
> Nor hence shall I budge, I've a notion,
> Nay, here shall my whistling and singing
> Set all His street's echoes a-ringing
> Long after the last of your number
> Has ceased my front-court to encumber . . .

This sounds like Billy Sunday scolding the Higher Critics. It reveals a blithe and vivacious piety which is peculiar to the Christian faith. One could not fancy a Hindu or a Buddhist chiding his critics with such boisterous good humour. It could, I think, be claimed that this overflow of joy at the rout of tragedy and tragedians is peculiar to orthodoxy. I have never found it in heresy. Heterodoxy is, of course, much nearer to the cold severity of mere religion. It may inspire a dry and acid wit, but not the capering gusto which really packs a wallop for pessimism. I had first noted this quality in Spurgeon, who wrote whole books full of jokes, puns and rough rhymes against social evils such as intemperance, misogyny and snobbish preachers. C. T. Studd bubbled over with it, declaring that to suffer is to be "ducked by the devil", but through faith we can always come up spluttering and say, "Sold again, old chap!" On the intellectual level this glee is exhibited in the dogmatic buffoonery of Chesterton and in some of Beverley Nichols' slapdash theological writings. Karl Barth has it too, especially in the *Epistle to the Romans*, where he is really wicked (!) in his use of interpolated exclamation marks which catch the reader like a dig in the ribs. All such writers are aware that Christianity does turn things upside down and that there is something quite dangerously frivolous about being a Christian.

3

I mentioned Barth's *Romans* specifically because it was at this period, in 1949, that I first read this earthquake of a book and gained from it a keener awareness of the impact of Christianity on man's tragic fate as a sinner. The book awed and shook me as it has awed and shaken thousands of theological students. I already accepted the main points of its theology, but as I bore its seismic heavings and buffetings I became even more concerned about my position as an outsider. I was severely challenged by Barth's passionate appeal for all Christians to take their stand openly in the Church and share its "guilt and its tribulation". I saw at a deeper level that the cross which the disciple is asked to bear for Christ's sake has no connection whatever with the natural ills which flesh is heir to. The heaviest cross we can carry is Christian belief itself—to believe that God has rejected man's righteousness and decided that he must be justified by grace or perish. This is more wounding to our pride than any amount of outward affliction. Many people who meekly accept a physical handicap as their cross are still determined to dodge the real cross of assent to the Christian verdict on man. Yet there can be no natural substitute for the Via Dolorosa of grace; it is the only pathway of discipleship.

When Christ said, "In the world ye shall have tribulations," he was not referring to personal and private disasters, for some Christians go through life unscathed by such things, and others endure them needlessly because they confuse their natural fate with God's will. Christ was speaking of the tribulation which is a direct result of faith, the result of being out of step with the thwarted earth and the fallen wisdom, out of step with man's self-righteousness. This spiritual pang and burden is inseparable from the sin and travail of the Church; it is always "turned into joy" and it stands in total contradiction to the sufferings of the world which, as Paul told the Corinthians, "worketh death". If we refuse to identify ourselves with the visible Church—the Church of Esau, as Barth calls it—in all its miserable defilement, we shall never apprehend the decision of God by which the Church of Esau becomes the Church of Jacob, the firstfruits of a New Creation. For it is with the guilt and tribulation of the Church that the possibility of human tragedy reaches its climax and is dissolved by grace. The highest achievement of "suffering humanity" is there met by the Cross and annihilated. "In the slain body of Christ we perceive the non-existence of men and supremely of religious (!) men." The Head of the Church brings its members under the redemptive decision of God, His arbitrary decision that Esau is Jacob, that the disinherited is the true heir, that the sinner is justified by faith. The door of hope is thereby opened to all mankind:

"Through the slain body of Christ, we are what we are not. Observed from this scene of death, 'we' live no

> more; we are dead to the law, dead to the possibility
> and necessity of religion, dead to every human pos-
> sibility; we are removed, set free, unfettered."[3]

This leads on to a recognition of the profoundest depths
of Christian truth, not exclusively Barthian. The Christian antidote to suffering demands the removal of all
"human possibilities" because of the original act of dis-
obedience from which all possibilities of human self-
expression have evolved. Every soul comes into the world
under sentence of death because of racial sin. That sentence is cancelled only by the Cross and in the paradox of
faith. Apart from the Cross, every soul would die in its
natural state and go to the eternal corruption which is
called hell. But the mercy of God has provided an alternative. By faith the soul can identify itself with Christ
and be "baptized into His death".[4] If it dies in nature it
stays dead; if it dies in Christ it shares His resurrection—
not only in a future state but here and now, in the process
of conversion. During great evangelistic campaigns hun-
dreds of people under sentence of spiritual death enter a
building, and emerge a few hours later with the sentence
executed, the resurrected life already glowing through
them. They face the future with the exultant affirmation
of St. Paul: "I am crucified with Christ: nevertheless I
live; yet not I, but Christ liveth in me."[5] This does not
exempt them from further trial—the resurrected life has
to contend with the world, the flesh and the devil; but
there is always the sense of a new control, a new pattern,
a fellowship with the tribulation of the Church.

The whole philosophy of Christian optimism is founded on the literal resurrection of Christ, the fact that His
triumph was a part of His earthly and corporeal existence. When those feet last walked our earth they were
not the feet of a sufferer, a Man of Sorrows. When that
voice last spoke it did not say, "My God, why has Thou
forsaken me?" The mask was dropped; the sufferings
were left behind with the moral precepts. The feet moved

briskly across the shore to a picnic in the spring dawn; the voice asked playfully: "Children, have ye any meat?" This is the truly revolutionary aspect of Christianity, and we must never let anything distract us from it—not even the Sermon on the Mount. The Christian ethic is revolutionary only if men translate it into action, but whether they trouble to do this or not, the central shock of the Christian revelation remains. The Second Person of the Trinity, killed by the depravity of man, became an unveiled physical reality beyond death, and granted His disciples glimpses of the New Creation of which He is Lord. It is sheer nonsense to argue, as Modernists do, that it does not matter whether Christ's resurrection was literal or spiritual. The nature of eternal reality and the evaluation of our whole temporal experience are at stake in this issue. In the drama of Redemption, God revealed His own character, the pattern He would have us follow. The pattern was either that of a Greek tragedy or that of a fairy-tale, and which it was depends on whether the cry of anguish was the last that was heard of Christ in this world or whether the cry was followed by a whimsical invitation to a breakfast on the beach. God must love tragedy more than comedy if He let His own flesh moulder into the soil of Palestine, but if He "took it again" as the first trophy in an attack on cosmic gloom, He has set the pace for an eternal comedy.

Almost all pessimistic philosophy in the Western world is associated with the denial of the literal resurrection of Christ. The survival of His teaching or His "Spirit" is not enough to confirm our shy hunger for the fairy-tale touch, nor does it shock us enough to be truly redemptive. It could take us no further than natural religion, the ascetic recoil from the permanent "grossness" of the flesh. The prospect of immortality must be as wan and dreary to us as it was to the ancient Greeks if we deny that the incarnate Son, with earthly food in His body, ascended beyond time and space, completing and consecrating for us the eternal unity of spirit and matter.

A merely spiritual resurrection would rob us of this unique Christian mystery; it would make the central mystery of Easter a cross and a silence. This creates a mass of artificial and depressing problems concerning the indifference or inaction of God, the apparent triumph of evil and so forth. T. F. Powys, in one of the darker passages of his *Soliloquies*, sums up what Easter must mean without the literal Resurrection:

> "It all leads to the Agony in the Garden. . . . We may well sorrow over the sorrows of our Lord, for one day the nails will be driven into our own hands. We pass our days as gaily as we can, but the book of our tragedy is in our doors: open it and know what we are and how we shall end."

James Russell Lowell, the Unitarian, could read only the same mournful lesson into the story of a rejected Messiah:

> Truth for ever on the scaffold,
> Wrong for ever on the throne.

The orthodox Christian holds an entirely different kind of philosophy because his thinking is based on much more cheerful premises. He insists that the nails and sorrows were *not* the end of the earthly pattern of reality which God revealed in Christ. Truth did not for ever stay on the scaffold: Truth came down from the scaffold, walked out of the tomb and ate boiled fish. This is where we catch the twinkle in God's eye and are privileged to enter the kingdom of a little child. Through the resurrection, we are purged of our corrupt adult taste for the "dignity" of pessimism and allowed to feel something of what Chesterton called "the frantic energy of divine things" which, as he says, would "knock us down like a drunken farce" if it were not sometimes tempered by our tears. The Empty Tomb proclaims that the fairy-tale formula is

God's norm, and the stature of every Christian must be measured by the extent to which his life is filled with incredible transformations of character and circumstance.

By this standard many Christian intellectuals are seen to be spiritual dwarfs compared with the simple believer. Here in Cornwall the shouting illiterate, Billy Bray, with his ecstatic witness to answered prayer towers above the scholarly Colenso, who was not ecstatic even about his amendment to the Noah's Ark story. No one is denied the wonders of the invading Kingdom on temperamental grounds: God's offer of a picnic beyond the nails and sorrow is made even to neurotic believers, but they often refuse it through fear of pride and continue to question amid the shadows. Kierkegaard's life might have been a Danish fairy-tale, but he preferred the more austere and philosophic rôle of martyrdom. I found it illuminating to contrast his experience with Elizabeth Barrett's. Both were physically unfit to marry, but God saw that for each of them marriage was essential if they were to bear witness to deliverance from the dark fate imposed by heredity. He made provision for both, sending Browning to Elizabeth Barrett, Regine Olsen to Kierkegaard. Elizabeth, after a long struggle with the proud demon of "renunciation", humbly accepted her liberty, thinking nothing of her own unworthiness but only of the mercy of God. Kierkegaard fought a similar battle, but lost it and died a frustrated bachelor because he could not surrender his view of himself as one ordained to interpret the sombre mystery of the Absolute. No one today can have any doubt as to which of these naturally tragic figures did the will of God. The man who renounced earthly happiness in order to seem more like the "historical Jesus" has cast a theological cloud—not of error but of truth darkened by personal misery—over thousands of minds. The woman who renounced suffering and escaped into what she called "my own especial fairy-tale"—the Resurrection pattern—set an example which has shone out like a beacon light for a century, enshrined in the most exultant love letters in English literature.

> "*I sat by while the angel stirred the water, and I called it* Miracle. *It is something to me between dream and miracle, all of it—as if some dream of my earliest brightest dreaming-time had been lying through these dark years to steep in the sunshine, returning to me in a double light. ... And now I must say this besides. When grief came upon grief, I never was tempted to ask 'How have I deserved this of God,' as sufferers sometimes do: I always felt that there must be cause enough ... corruption enough, needing purification ... weakness enough, needing strengthening ... nothing of the chastisement could come to me without cause and need. But in this different hour, when joy follows joy, and God makes me happy, as you say, through you ... I cannot repress the ... 'How have I deserved this of Him?'—I know I have not—I know I do not.*
>
> *Could it be that heart and life were devastated to make room for you?—If so it was well done ... dearest! They leave the ground fallow before the wheat.*"[6]

In such a passage we hear the music of an eternal truth more profound and moving than anything that can be reached through mere suffering. It puts to shame the tragic outcries of Kierkegaard's *Journal* and the curt, self-torturing asceticism of Simone Weil. This awareness of the perfect fusion of Providence and grace, of flesh and spirit subdued to the joyous predestination of God—this is indeed the rout of tragedy and the most complete witness to the Gospel which "breaks the power of cancelled sin, and sets the prisoner free".

[1] 2 Corinthians 5: 17.
[2] Hebrews 1: 9.
[3] *Epistle to the Romans*, p. 234.
[4] Romans 6: 3.
[5] Galatians 2: 20.
[6] The Browning Love Letters, vol. 1, p. 285.

CHAPTER EIGHT

THE BRIDGEHEAD AND BEYOND

Whom He did predestinate, them He also called: and whom He called, them He also justified: and whom He justified, them He also glorified.

St. Paul

O that all might catch the flame,
All partake the glorious bliss!

Charles Wesley

I

The reader will probably have noticed that the word "Calvinism" is used very sparingly in the foregoing pages. The Press and radio comment on my earlier books has sometimes made me wish I had never called myself a Calvinist. My creed has not changed, but the term "Calvinism" gives a distorted idea of it to those who are not well acquainted with theological movements. A Christian who affirms the sterner truths of the Faith is always liable to misrepresentation, and unless the false statements are corrected they may destroy the effectiveness of his whole work. When C. S. Lewis championed providential discipline in *The Problem of Pain* he said it did not matter that he himself should seem monstrous in the eyes of the hostile reader, but it mattered enormously if he should "alienate anyone from the truth". I have come to feel much the same about the defence of the doctrine of election. There could be no doubt that the interpretation placed upon it in some quarters would tend to alienate people from the Scriptural teaching I wished them to see. The public was informed that I believed in "a tyrannical deity interested only in His favourites" and was engaged in "a narrower and more ruthless teaching than anything in Lawrence". Such verdicts made me realize that no good purpose would be served by drawing attention to my Calvinism, thus enabling critics to dodge the challenge of my Christianity.

It may help to clear up further misunderstanding if I briefly summarize the main points of my personal creed.

The Biblical ideas which have influenced me most may be roughly grouped as follows:

1. That every human being has a tragic destiny in nature and a (potential) triumphant one in Divine grace.
2. That this higher destiny is the "new and living way" opened up by the Incarnation, Atonement and Resurrection of Christ.
3. That conversion involves a "leap of faith" from nature to grace.
4. That in every generation a certain number of individuals, called in Scripture the elect, are compelled by God to make this leap in order to form the nucleus or bridgehead of faith for that generation.
5. That while the higher destiny of eternal life is offered to the non-elect, they must voluntarily accept it.

That is my "Calvinism"—the formula that underlines my fiction and poetry. It has obvious affinities with the Barthian doctrine of "double predestination", and there are echoes of Spurgeon, Browning and Kierkegaard. But I have never slavishly followed any human teacher. I am concerned only that my theology should be in complete harmony with the Word of God and the facts of observation and experience.

My belief in the reality of fate does not make me a

fatalist. I do not believe that "what is to be will be" in the depressing sense of the phrase. What God has promised He will certainly perform for all who have entered into covenant with Him, but those who are not yet in the covenant may come in by an act of faith and thereby change the whole course of their future lives. The essence of the Christian Gospel lies in its proclamation to the individual: "Your fate is unspeakably tragic, *but you need not fulfil it*. Surrender the self that would fulfil that fate and the fate itself collapses. You become a new creature with a new destiny." That is their heritage in Christ—escape from the dark, slimy coils of what nature has decreed for us. On the natural level fate is inexorable and relentless: the greatest geniuses have not been able to break its stranglehold with all their frantic efforts of mind and will. Only one thing ever has broken it, and that is the impact of Divine grace working through the forgiveness of sins.

There are few pleasures of the Kingdom more satisfying than the sense of release from fate. If I can judge from my own reactions there are times when every Christian feels rather like a naughty child who has played truant. He is not where his stern mother, Dame Nature, meant him to be: he is not obeying the laws which a fallen spiritual world demands that he should obey: he is not learning the arts of self-expression and self-fulfilment for which he was originally designed as a sinner. He is expressing and fulfilling something else, something incredibly strange—the Will of God. He has been drawn apart with Christ to explore the enchanted ground of the personal covenant—not to enjoy it selfishly, but to add another facet of witness to Christianity as the divine "way of escape" without which mankind must remain trapped in the hard and profitless school of natural experience. There is a constant knowledge that natural integrity, the honesty of the "old Adam", has been violated, yet the rebel feels, as William James put it, "consciously right, superior and happy".

In all my books, and most of my other writings, I have tried to embody this concept of the triumph of faith over fate, but the critics persisted in describing it as a harsh and inhuman dogma. One reviewer even referred to my "black Calvinism". He might as truly have called the sun black because it shines on a slag-heap! My natural vision was indeed a slag-heap thrown out from the spent fires of paganism, but the faith which exposed and finally dissolved it was as buoyant as Browning's, as exuberant as Chesterton's, as fervid as Vachel Lindsay's. How can any faith be harsh or inhuman which draws its power from the Resurrection by which the salvation of some men was made certain and the salvation of all others made possible? It seemed clear that the charges were due to the critic's ignorance of theological movements. To them the word "Calvinism" had not changed its meaning since the eighteenth century. It denoted the creed which had driven Cowper mad and caused the Scottish people to sit in frozen fatalism, convinced that if they were elect they would go to heaven, willy-nilly, and if they were not elect they would be damned anyhow, so why make any effort to believe? This perversion had receded during the nineteenth century under the influence of liberal Calvinists like Spurgeon, Talmage and Alexander Whyte; not a trace of it survived into the twentieth century. The great modern Calvinistic thinkers—Barth, Brunner and Niebuhr—would endorse Charles Wesley's vehement rejoinder to the hyper-Calvinist of his day:

> For all my Lord was crucified—
> For all, for all, my Saviour died.

And that is my position. There is no negative side to my concept of predestination for the word is never used negatively in the New Testament. It always affirms the triumph of God's gracious and loving purpose: "Whom He did foreknow, He also did predestinate to be conformed to the image of His Son."[1] No one could be predestinated to damnation, since predestination operates only where God foreknows that there is faith. Many people make the mistake of regarding predestination and fate as synonymous. They may be synonymous to Mohammedans and non-Christian philosophers, but to the Christian they are as opposite as grace and nature. Christian predestination is God's bright *alternative* to the darkness of natural fate. The latter is mentioned in Scripture only as the general condemnation of man in Adam. Jude declares that the impenitent non-elect will suffer the doom to which, as natural creatures, they were "ordained"—and to which every other human being since the fall has been ordained. St. Paul admits that the elect are "by nature the children of wrath, even as others".[2] They are redeemed from this nature, and from the fate imposed by it, so that others may be shown the way of escape.

This truth is brought out distinctly in Christ's high priestly prayer in the seventeenth chapter of St. John's Gospel. He claims to have received "power over all flesh, that He should give eternal life to as many as Thou hast given Him". These are sharply distinguished from the non-elect "world": "I pray not for the world, but for those whom Thou hast given me out of the world." A few verses further on, however, Christ says that the elect are chosen and sanctified "that the world may believe". God wants the rest of mankind to be added to the elect nucleus, who represent in mature spiritual form the idea expressed in the Old Testament by the choice of Israel as a channel of blessing to the Gentiles.

The concept of a wholly benevolent predestination is not, of course, confined to neo-Calvinism. It is the official teaching of the Church of England as defined in its seventeenth Article of Belief. Theodor Haecker, in his book *Kierkegaard the Cripple*, puts forward the Roman Catholic view to refute Kierkegaard's too extreme reaction against the harsh dualism of Geneva:

"Kierkegaard had a healthy horror of Calvin's teaching

of the predestination of the damned ... but he over-
looked in his anxiety the numerous references in Scrip-
ture to the predestination of the saints and chosen ones.
This means that God loves all men, and this is the solid
foundation of all Christian theology, but He does not
love all equally, but some more than others."

The principle of a divine choice of individuals for a special work or purpose is often explicit in the New Testament. In the tenth chapter of Acts, for instance, we are told that the resurrected body of Christ was shown "not unto all the people, but unto all the witnesses chosen before of God". The fact that a handful of Jews were arbitrarily selected to behold the risen Lord did not deprive anyone else of an assurance of the Resurrection. Christ actually said to one of these favoured witnesses: "Because thou hast seen thou hast believed: Blessed are they which have not seen and yet have believed." In other words, blessed are the non-elect who obey without compulsion; blessed is the ordinary convert who signs his decision card and then walks by faith and not by sight. All down through the ages the elect witnesses have received special manifestations both in Providential workings and on the psychic level, but this has meant enrichment, not deprivation, to the mass of average Christians who are not granted such spectacular proofs. The example of the great Crusaders is a challenge which often leads some obscure believer to covenant with God for some little blessing in his own sphere—something which does not make Church history or newspaper headlines, but is valid as a token of God's faithfulness.

Most modern evangelists and orthodox writers by-pass the idea of an elect minority because it raises such acute problems concerning divine justice and the relation between the sovereignty of God and man's free will. Many attempts have been made to cut the knot. Henry Ward Beecher suggested that "the elect are whosoever will, the non-elect whosoever won't". This is an improvement on

Calvin's rigid determinism, but it is invalidated by the fact that some Christians backslide and become apostates. If all Christians were elect there could be no apostates, for the eternal security of the elect is guaranteed in dozens of New Testament texts. Apostasy occurs only among non-elect believers, to whom Christ's warnings about the barren branches of the vine and the salt which has lost its savour, are applicable. The elect are not perfect, they are not exempt from moods of depression, perplexity and spiritual dryness, but they always avail themselves of the infinite resources of Christ's power and fight through to victory. The same provision is made for the non-elect, but they often neglect it, despite warnings, and fall back once more to the level of their natural fate. Even then the grace of repentance is offered them, and the divine pursuit continues. Some non-elect Christians backslide and repent, only to backslide again, so that their earthly lives are a pitiful confusion in which the divine plan is seen only at rare intervals: triumphs are followed by disasters because faith and obedience were not maintained.

The doctrine of election is essential to an understanding of Christian strategy, but it is balanced by other Bible truths and does not tend to foster egoism or complacency in the individual. We can recognize the men of destiny who mark turning-points in the history of Christendom, but only God knows absolutely who is eternally secure and who is not. We always have to reckon with His love of paradox, His determination that the last shall be first and the first shall be last. A man's spiritual status cannot be judged by the nature of his work. God is completely free to elect a film star or a gipsy, while deciding that a bishop shall be a non-elect believer who may apostatize and perish. A person may be elect without being a chosen instrument for some spectacular task, and those who are called to such tasks dare not be presumptuous. No one could be more obviously a "chosen vessel" than St. Paul, yet he realized that he must be vigilant, "lest, that by any means, when I have preached to others, I myself should be a castaway".[3] This is a healthy attitude, and every Christian should submit himself to the searching of God's Word and resolve that, whether he is elect or not, he will be among those who hold fast to the end and inherit the Kingdom where the distinction between elect and non-elect believers will disappear, and there shall be "one fold and one Shepherd".

This Scriptural form of Calvinism is a great stimulus to Christian humility. No Calvinist can be proud, for a man must have been granted an almost frantic humility if he believes he is totally depraved, that his natural religious insight is part of his tragic fate, that the judgment of God has already condemned everything he can naturally think, say or do, and that he is justified only by the imputed righteousness of Christ. These Pauline truths are the strongest defence I know against the dreadful humanist theology that switches the emphasis from God to man, stressing not what God has done for us but what we can do for God, not His election of men as sinners but their election of Him as a Being who conforms fairly well to their idea of what a good God ought to be like. Such arrogance is one of the worst expressions of depravity, for it rejects grace on religious ground. As Browning declared in *Saul*, divine grace will not "leave up nor down one spot for the creature to stand in". At the crisis of surrender all "creaturely" positions must be evacuated and the sovereignty of God acknowledged in its redemptive aspect alone. For every Christian, whether he is a chosen instrument or an obscure believer, grace must be the flood-tide of consciousness and the all-pervading memory must be the memory of the forgiveness of sins.

2

Looking back now over thirty years of Christian experience, I can say that my dominant aim has been to do some pioneering work around the contemporary bridge-head of faith, repairing the breach and restoring the paths of Evangelical doctrine and Christian marriage. I have been privileged to do some recognizable part of my covenant task through books, magazines and radio programmes. If I have strayed into by-ways of mysticism I have at least learnt that mysticism is not a mark of election or even of surrender. As my faith matures I find myself less and less responsive to the speculative mystic. These tranquil visionaries, from Boehme and Traherne to Trine and Tagore, can make little contact with a restless, crusading spirit. Contemplation is too near to natural piety to have much place in a Christian's devotional life. A critic once described me as being akin to the monks "who sought out holes in the rocks for meditation", but he had read too much into a few passages written under T. F. Powys's influence. Only in times of spiritual debility have I given myself to religious brooding. I experimented with many moods and methods, but the only ones that have value today are those which brought me nearest to the revivalist world.

Our Lord compared Christian witness to a "city set on a hill", and I have felt increasingly that all its neon signs should be blazing to arrest the strugglers in the dark valley—including the natural mystic. The dim light in the cloister is an absolute symbol: it was always a morbid and degenerate symbol for true Christian light is flaming and spectacular and even a bit garish, like St. John's picture of heaven. The wholesome idea of the Christian saint and visionary is expressed by the hot-gospeller rather than the wistful pietist. I would not despise the spiritual illumination of sufferers, but whenever I have tried to share it the result has been unhealthy and perverse. I have therefore rejected it as inimical to the type of witness that is needed in this seething modern age. Religious stunts organized by human ingenuity are signs of impotence but God's chosen vessels of revival will be led to do things which conventional people will mistake for stunts. As Christianity is God's foolishness invading man's wisdom, God's joy invading man's despair, it is God's colour and excitement invading man's wicked taste for drab and dignified piety.

This bias towards sensationalism may sometimes spring from a kind of Evangelical mysticism—the psychic awareness of a supernatural "call" which vitalized Luther and Spurgeon and is the driving force behind several modern American fire-brands. If this can be called mystical election I might admit to having some sympathy with it, for the power that made me articulate for the Gospel despite my natural destiny as a pagan dreamer—this belongs to the same Pentecostal category. It is not just a literary talent, for it will function only on the stimulus of faith. I write only because I believe—and I write now explicitly from within the Christian fellowship, I have not yet been guided to join a denomination, but since 1950 I have worshipped with orthodox Christians of various types and have given spiritual and practical support to many evangelistic movements. In 1953 the threat of physical handicaps led me to seek divine healing, and this involved my acceptance of the Anglo-Catholic rite of confession and absolution. I did not think it necessary, but the priest did, and I felt that a little humble submission on my part would do no harm. My personal bias has remained Nonconformist. In August 1955 I took the decisive step of communion, receiving the sacrament of the Lord's Supper from a Methodist minister who became my friend while stationed in Cornwall, and for a decade after this I received the sacrament occasionally from his successors. Since my marriage in 1968 I have attended my old village chapel regularly. I do not favour the organic merging of denominations, but in 1969 my wife and I took part in a procession to the parish church when a mission was launched there by the diocesan Bishop.

My affinities are with those in all the churches who affirm God in Christ with the full traditional implications.

I have outgrown any kinship I have ever had with people who are merely "religious", people who claim that they are worshipping God in their own way and that He is congratulating them on their integrity. I agree with C. S. Lewis that such an individualistic creed is "under God's curse and will (apart from God's grace) lead those who believe it to eternal death".[4] It is good that this uncompromising stand has been taken again—and not only by a "harsh Calvinist"!—after the long lapse into heresies which were at least as sentimental as mysticism. Church members are beginning to wake up from the torpor of Modernism, really coming alive, really caring about Truth. And as a result the outsiders are coming to feel their need of the Shepherd, the pastor and the fellowship.

The resurgence of true evangelism spreads always from the elect bridgehead of faith, which is established in every generation as a divine guarantee that Christian truth shall never be dislodged from this rebellious planet. The victory of God is therefore assured at least within the boundary of election, and this fact corrects the pessimism of the Arminian's view that all mankind is free to reject Christ or perish. If no one were elect it would be difficult to feel hopeful about the future of Christianity. For centuries its basic doctrines have been regarded by most educated people as obsolete, and with every major advance of science comes the prophecy that the Christian religion has received its death-blow. So far these predictions have been falsified, and those who fail to note the law of election which is operating here must be perplexed, not only by the survival of the old Gospel but by its ability to burst upon a new generation with all the freshness and vigour of something that has just been discovered along with television and the hydrogen bomb.

I remember reading in a literary paper just before my conversion, an article which solemnly posed the question: "Are we witnessing to the passing of Christianity?" The writer was very sympathetic, very regretful at the decline of traditional beliefs, but he had little doubt that the orthodox concepts were crumbling into oblivion. God's eye must have twinkled as He read this obituary, for He was soon to lay His hand on a number of men through whom a completely orthodox Christianity was to renew its impact during or after the Second World War. I refer to such figures as C. S. Lewis, D. R. Davies, C. E. M. Joad, Thomas Merton, Billy Graham and Oral Roberts. I include the Trappist monk, Merton, because in his best-selling book, *Elected Silence*, he showed all the signs of being a chosen witness to supernatural grace as it works destructively on the foundations of modern humanism. Graham and Roberts must obviously be mentioned, for though their approach was often regarded as superficial and, in the case of Roberts, lacking in doctrinal precision, they led evangelism to some of the most spectacular heights it has ever reached: Graham's mammoth crusades in Western capitals jolted complacent heathens both outside and inside the churches. Through the mid-century consecration of these widely differing personalities, the "passing of Christianity" was indefinitely postponed, and those who would have been somewhat relieved to see it replaced by a natural religion were left to squeal about the "menace" of traditional thought-forms.

It is the hidden principle of election that confounds the pessimist, and renews to the Church the vitality of its first love and restores hope to the world. However apostate the Church may be, however formidable the opposition from political systems or scientific hypotheses, there is always "a remnant according to the election of grace",[5] and the gates of hell cannot prevail against it. To every chosen vessel the promise is fulfilled, spiritually and theologically: "A thousand shall fall at thy side, and ten thousand at thy right hand; but it shall not come nigh thee."[6] During the period when Christianity seemed to be passing, thousands of Christians fell under the assault of various heresies—Darwinism, Higher Criticism, Christian Socialism and the New Psychology. But amid the wastage the elect remnant testified to an unscathed Gospel, they stood steadfast and immovable, custodians of the foolishness of God. The light and energy of this invading foolishness exist on earth as a witness rather than a dominion, for Christ's Kingdom is not of this world. Through the Church, human history is beset and illuminated by the eternal Word, but none of its major kindling in the past has succeeded in converting a whole nation. During the great Wesleyan revival multitudes of English people remained unregenerate. The Methodists built their chapels, but the gaols, taverns and brothels remained full, cruelty and squalor abounded, and continued to abound all through the nineteenth century while Moody, Spurgeon and General Booth preached and laboured. Nor does the New Testament lead us to expect that all human sin will ever cease through the spreading of the Gospel. Christ did not promise the sort of results which idealists have in mind. Even the Beatitudes were qualified by a grim realism: having said "Blessed are the peacemakers", He jolted our complacency by adding, "Ye shall hear of wars."[7] All attempts to achieve righteousness as a human possibility are doomed to failure, and though the divine possibility is offered it is rejected by millions, century after century. Until the end of time Christians will have to affirm with St. John: "We know that we are of God, and the whole world lieth in wickedness."[8] But a revival does vastly increase the number of those who receive the truth; it does extend the spiritual rule of Christ outside the elect bridgehead and thereby lessen the area of wickedness in the world. Those who do not surrender are disturbed by hints of something behind the mask of the Nazarene, behind the foolishness of the Cross, something awesome and inescapable, even now in their midst—the glory and grandeur of the redeeming God. Above all, a revival cleanses and strengthens the Church as an instrument of witness to the supernatural Kingdom which will at last be manifested in the stupendous act of divine sensationalism, the Second Coming. That is the climax of the invasion, the point of final cleavage between grace and judgment, towards which mankind was inexorably set moving by the Incarnation.

It is significant that at the time of my recovery from isolationism the attack on heresy within the Church was being made most vigorously by the younger Christians. There was a reversal of the position which had been almost taken for granted thirty years before. During my childhood orthodox parents were usually grieved to see their children swept away by popular scepticism, but in the 'fifties it was often the sceptical parents who were grieved—or at least exasperated—to find that their children had progressed so far beyond them as to reach orthodoxy again. It could be said that orthodoxy had become the fashion among young converts, and if it could be a fashion of this world the widespread movement towards it by Christians under forty might reflect only a swing of the pendulum from one extreme to another. But orthodoxy is the Gospel of the eternal Kingdom, and in accepting it people are merely obeying the New Testament command to "fashion yourself according to the coming transformation".[9] By it they enter the innermost sanctuary of Christian truth and find that this too is a paradox. The sanctuary is the seat of the divine disturbance, the point from which God reached out to shake the nests in the waste-land. Signs of this shaking, this pledge of the coming transformation, are still apparent in spite of the drugs of sex-mysticism and the fog-belts of so-called radical thinking. By various methods, from the analytical brilliance of Francis Schaeffer to the forthright testimony of Cliff Richards, people are being stabbed into awareness that the old truth remains valid, that it is invading them and stirring their nests.

It has invaded me completely. I have entered its sanctuary and taken its sacrament and no longer launch out from a private nest among the clay-peaks. Every facet of my natural self—the pagan mystic, the brooding hermit, the baffled individualist—is gone without trace. I have been filled with the joy of the maturing convert who has given his natural fate the slip by surrendering all its possibilities to the Divine Invader. I was never allowed to find contentment either in exile or in my individualist vision of Christian truth. Even while my back was towards the sanctuary the cry of Donne had been wrung from me amid the sensual or aesthetic shadows:

> Burn off my rust and my deformity!
> Renew Thine image so much, by Thy grace,
> That Thou mayest know me; and I'll turn my face.

The breadth and fullness of the renewal were very striking on that afternoon when my wife and I took part in the church procession. I was still a complex poet, and scores of housewives, labourers and tradesmen marched with me, but the difference had ceased to matter as the jaunty strains of the village band floated away over the sunlit churchyard.

1 Romans 8: 29.
2 Ephesians 2: 3.
3 1 Corinthians 9: 27.
4 *Broadcast Talks.*
5 Romans 11: 5.
6 Psalm 91: 7.
7 Matthew 24: 6.
8 1 John 5: 19.
9 *Romans* 12: 2 (Barth's translation).